*

Advertising and New Media

Consumers around the world are rapidly incorporating new networked media and communications into their daily lives and, in the process, are acquiring new forms and capacities of control and influence in their negotiations with the media.

Advertising and New Media tracks this shift from 'mass' to 'my' media and considers how conversational interaction and social participation are reshaping the social relations of media service providers, advertisers and consumers.

Christina Spurgeon provides a clear and comprehensive introduction to the co-evolutionary development of advertising, new media and new media consumers, with examples drawn from the USA, the UK, Europe, Australia and the People's Republic of China.

Features include:

- evaluation of consumer-generated advertising, including the Coke Mentos phenomenon, and comparative analysis of the Dove 'Real Beauty' and Axe/Lynx 'Effect' campaigns;
- interviews with industry practitioners, providing first-hand insights on the impact of new media on advertising;
- tables and figures that support differentiated analyses of the impact of changing media consumption patterns on mass media.

Christina Spurgeon lectures in Journalism, Media and Communication in the Creative Industries Faculty at the Queensland University of Technology and is an active, published researcher and public interest advocate in media and communication industries and policy. Christina has previously worked as a radio producer and journalist specializing in 'media on media', and as a media and communications researcher and public policy adviser.

Advertising and New Media

Christina Spurgeon

LONDON AND NEW YORK

First published 2008
by Routledge
2 Park Square, Milton Park, Abingdon, Oxon OX14 4RN

Simultaneously published in the USA and Canada
by Routledge
270 Madison Ave, New York, NY 10016

Routledge is an imprint of the Taylor & Francis Group, an informa business

Typeset in Perpetua by
Book Now Ltd, London
Printed and bound in Great Britain by
CPI Antony Rowe, Chippenham, Wiltshire

British Library Cataloguing in Publication Data
A catalogue record for this book is available from the British Library

Library of Congress Cataloging in Publication Data
Spurgeon, Christina.
Advertising and new media / Christina Spurgeon.
p. cm.
Includes bibliographical references and index.
1. Internet advertising. 2. Advertising. 3. Advertising–Social aspects.
4. Mass media. 5. Mass media and business. I. Title.

HF6146.I58S68 2007
659.13'4–dc22 2007020168

ISBN10: 0–415–43034–8 (hbk)
ISBN10: 0–415–43035–6 (pbk)
ISBN10: 0–203–93552–7 (ebk)

ISBN13: 978–0–415–43034–0 (hbk)
ISBN13: 978–0–415–43035–7 (pbk)
ISBN13: 978–0–203–93552–1 (ebk)

Contents

Acknowledgements

Many people have helped make this book possible. I am especially grateful to Sal Humphreys, Phil Graham and Alan McKee for their comments on drafts; to Adam Swift, Jenny Burton, Jiannu Bao, Cal Gilmour and Cathy Henkel for research assistance rendered along the way; to the Creative Industries Faculty at the Queensland University of Technology for supporting this research; to my colleagues in Journalism, Media and Communication for their encouragement and good will; and to my advertising students for their keen interest in this topic. I am also indebted to John Hartley, Stuart Cunningham, Michael Keane, Terry Flew, Graeme Turner, John Sinclair, Joanne Jacobs and Gerard Goggin for the benefit of their support and expertise at various times throughout this project; and to the many media and marketing communication scholars and industry professionals who so generously shared with me their insights on advertising and new media. I am also very thankful to my partner in life, Stephen Thompson, for many things including his outstanding work on the manuscript, and to my wonderful daughter Lucy for her good humour and patience.

Chapter 1

Advertising and the new media of mass conversation

Home videos of explosive Coke–Mentos soda fountains and Coke–Mentos rockets started appearing on the Web in early 2006. This association of Coke with a lesser known brand of mints took both brands by surprise. The brand companies could control neither the uses made of their products, nor the dissemination of the images of these uses. The replication, video capture and Web-based sharing of Coke–Mentos experiments snowballed. Thousands of experiments were uploaded to the Web and viewed by millions. A very enterprising team of performance artists called EepyBird took the Coke–Mentos phenomenon to new aesthetic heights. One particular experiment, which commentators likened to the spectacular fountains of the Bellagio Hotel in Las Vegas, was rapidly powered up by virally-disseminated, viewer-generated recommendations to the top of 'most watched' lists on sites such as Revver and YouTube.[1] Mentos was very happy with this popular appropriation and display of its brand, and its association with youth culture values. It estimated this media exposure was worth US$10 million, equivalent to more than half its annual advertising budget for the US market (Vranica and Terhune 2006), and took immediate steps to build on this publicity opportunity by partnering with YouTube to run a competition for the best Coke–Mentos video. Although early responses reported from Coke were not enthusiastic, the global soft drink giant also elected to explore this consumer-generated media activity as a brand-building opportunity. It mounted a 'Poetry in Motion' competition that challenged Coke consumers to show the world what extraordinary things they could do with everyday objects (Vranica and Terhune 2006).

The Coke–Mentos experiments cut right to the heart of the challenge that new media present for advertising. Historically, advertisers have thought of themselves as top-down communicators, in control of what information is released, to whom and when, as well as the channels of communication themselves (Varey 2002). The Coke–Mentos experiments point to the ways in which new media stress this model of communication. They provide an iconic illustration of how and why advertisers, media and advertising industries, are increasingly compelled to think about new media consumers as key creative participants in advertising, media and marketing processes. The Coke–Mentos experiments could not be discounted as the antics of culture jammers or the interventions of anti-globalization activists. They are proof positive that audiences are actively involved in the 'management of media culture' (Arvidsson 2006: 74), prescribing new kinds of ambiences, goals and procedures for consumer interaction, participation and productivity. That is the central argument of this book – that new media based on information and communication technologies (ICTs), such as the internet and cell phones, invite us to think in exciting new ways about advertising, as an industry and marketing communication process, as well as a crucially important influence in consumer and public culture.

This chapter frames this development as a shift from mass media to the new media of mass conversation. Mass media are the communication services of mass society, mass production and consumption. Niche media tailor these services to market segments, often on a global scale. Conversational media are the communication services of the global network economy and information society. They overlay rather than supersede mass and niche media, and, as the older media forms are digitized, conversational media also augment and converge with mass media to produce new, niche and one-to-one media forms. The Coke–Mentos experiments illuminate the co-adaptive development of advertising and media, another important theme of this book. They also point to the myriad ways in which new media uses can rapidly reorganize the social relations of media production, commercial communication and consumer markets. In the first instance, people are no longer as dependent on mass media for information and entertainment. As personal computers and fixed and mobile network connections multiply, reaching the point of ubiquity in many parts of the world, the density of networked conversations increases. Convergent developments in consumer electronics and social software that support peer-to-peer interaction also cause the economic barriers to media production and distribution to plummet. A variety of new commercial media, which take advantage of the conversational productivity of consumers, now extend the range of media choices well beyond mass and niche media. Examples, case studies, interviews with advertising industry professionals, and applied stakeholder analysis, are used throughout this book to draw attention to the impact of these changes in advertising and advertiser-funded media industries, audiences and texts.

Conversational media are both the consequences and drivers of the new economies of information and networks. They are being used to increase the variety of patterns of interaction and forms of social exchange, organization and politics. The important distinction between conversational interaction, which is taken here to be a cybernetic property of new media and communication systems, and dialogic exchange, which is characteristic of human communication and social participation, is developed in this chapter. Corresponding with the internet's rapid development as a platform for advertising and commerce, conversational views of interaction and participation have increasingly called into question the status of transmission as the natural systemic and social order of media. These developments, both at the coalface of advertising and media industries and in new media and marketing communication scholarship, are discussed throughout this book, as is their impact on the co-adaptation of advertising and new media.

Advertisers and their agencies often talk about the need to 'break through' the clutter of advertising-saturated media environments in order to command the attention of the consumers they want to reach. This is a problem of top-down transmission. As the Coke–Mentos case illustrates, conversational media can also cut through from the bottom up. Online chatter about Coke–Mentos experiments and the first visual demonstrations appear to have initially circulated in niche media and internet-based knowledge communities dedicated to popularizing and promoting science education. Viewer response finally 'broke through' to the brands after the extraordinary EepyBird Coke–Mentos experiments were uploaded to Revver. A consensus quickly emerged among Revver consumer critics about the outstanding entertainment qualities of the EepyBird work. It was at this point that the EepyBird team caught the attention of the brands, as well as mass media, and added further fuel to a wider conversation in professional marketing communication networks about the role of consumer-generated brand communications in marketing strategies (Prescott 2006; Sandoval 2006; Vranica and Terhune 2006).

Like YouTube, Current TV and numerous other video-sharing sites, Revver makes it easy for viewer-generated recommendations to circulate in the social networks of the internet. In addition to letting viewers rate content, the Revver site automatically generates code, which visitors painlessly copy and paste into their own blogs, email and websites, so that others may easily access content hosted by Revver. There is a great deal of variety in the detail of the business models underpinning these new services. Revver is distinguished by its dedication to ensuring that content producers – professional and amateur – can earn advertising income as they build audiences for their content, and keep control of their intellectual property. Each clip logged with Revver is tagged with advertising that is charged on a 'click through' basis. Revenue is split evenly between the video maker and Revver. The EepyBird team reportedly earned about US$30,000 from this arrangement prior to being picked up by the brands (Adegoke 2006).

The Revver business model is not a serious threat to the highly capital-intensive, top-down, approaches to financing production and distribution of the global media and entertainment industries. Rather, it is complementary. It illustrates how new, conversationally-inspired media diversify and extend the strategies available to independent content producers to include bottom-up approaches for building markets and attracting investor interest. Revver is one of a proliferating number of interesting and important instances of the co-adaptation of advertising and new media to conversational possibilities of interaction and participation.

The production of audiences for sale to advertisers, facilitated by the irresistible 'free lunch' of programme and editorial content, is at the heart of the advertising-funded media business model (Smythe 1981: 25). That imperative still operates in new commercial media. In this respect, there are important similarities between the new conversational and transmission media. Both principally rely on revenue earned from advertising and marketing services. However, there are also important differences. New media audiences cannot be conceived of as passive consumers of these services. Indeed, their active participation, especially as content creators, is a crucial ingredient of commercial success. In new media environments, revenues for advertising and marketing services are applied differently, to support the smorgasbord of communication tools essential to generating mass conversation media content (Marshall 2004: 59). Another striking difference is the way that people learn about mass conversation media. Sometimes a media report or standard media campaign will be the first source of news. More often than not, however, information about new conversation media is spread virally by electronic word-of-mouth.

Conversational interactivity and social participation

Although usually very loosely applied, interactivity has been a key category of comparison between 'old' mass media and 'new' digitally networked media (Burnett and Marshall 2003: 51–2). Henry Jenkins very usefully argues that in new media contexts interactivity is more precisely understood as a property of the technical systems of communication (Jenkins 2006: 133). Interaction is engineered. It can be broadly understood as the cybernetic control of information flows, including feedback, in any given communications system. The more interactive a communication system is, the more flexibility and variation in the types of communication and exchange it can support. The internet is considered the most interactive of all communication media because it is engineered to support all modes of interpersonal, mass and computer-mediated communication. Burnett and Marshall describe the interactive adaptability and flexibility of the internet as the 'loose web of communication' (Burnett and Marshall 2003: 45).

Strictly speaking, interactivity is a property of engineered systems of communication. However, it has been extended analogously to encompass physical media too, such as newspapers and magazines. One of the most influential typologies of systemic interactivity was proposed by Bordewijk and van Kaam in the mid-1980s as an aid to thinking about the policy and regulatory implications of ICTs. It relied on 'idealized information traffic patterns' to generate a scheme for differentiating the interactive properties and associated social relations of various media and communication services and networks, both analogue and digital (Bordewijk and van Kaam 2003). As Table 1.1 indicates, it establishes 'conversation' as an important type of mediated interactivity.

Bordewijk and van Kaam describe the one-to-many architecture of modern broadcast mass media as 'allocution'. This is the least responsive type of interactivity because it is not designed to support exchanges between the small number of powerful transmitters at the centre of allocutionary media and communication systems and the mass of media receivers. Nor does it support interaction between receivers. The one-way flow of information is under the programmatic control of the media service provider. Audiences do not generally represent themselves in the social relations of allocution. They are more likely to be represented in, and by, these systems in a variety of ways that are beyond the direct control of audiences. Audiences can turn broadcast media on and off and change channels. Remote controls and VCRs also significantly extended audience control over broadcast media (Varan interview 2005). There is, however, no feedback channel built into allocutionary media. This does not mean that these media lack interactivity. Rather, it is necessary to augment them in other ways, for example through audience measurement systems and marketing surveys, and by embedding telephone-based interactivity into programming (Nightingale and Dwyer 2006; Spurgeon and Goggin 2007; Gould 2007).

The type of interaction supported by newspapers, magazines and multichannel television services is described as 'consultation' because consumers exercise programmatic control in selecting information from a predetermined menu of content, often for the cost of a one-off purchase or an ongoing subscription. As with allocution, control is centralized. Peer-to-peer interaction is not supported and audiences are generally indirectly represented in the content and social

Table 1.1 Typology of cybernetic interaction

Type of Interaction	*Pattern of information flow*	*Location of programmatic control*	*Social relations*	*Example*
Allocution	One-to-many	Core	Representative	Broadcast media
Consultation	One-to-many	Periphery	Representative	Print media
Conversation	One-to-one	Periphery	Participatory	Telephone
Registration	One-to-one	Core	Representative	Subscription media; utilities
Digital	Multi-patterned	Dynamic	Representative; participatory; intercreative	Internet; cell phone

Source: adapted from Bordewijk and van Kaam 2003; Meilke 2002.

relations of these media. As with allocutionary media, the lack of in-built feedback loops is remediated through other systems.

'Conversation' describes the reciprocal patterns of interaction that occur in telephone and telecommunications networks. Control in conversational systems is far more distributed than in either allocution or consultation. Anyone connected to the network can initiate or terminate an interaction at any time with anyone else in the network. Consumers of these systems are more actively configured as users than as passive audiences or readerships because these communication media rely on participation and direct representation. This type of interactivity is of particular interest in this discussion, and is one to which I frequently return.

Telecommunications networks and subscription media also exhibit the functionality of another type of interactivity, which Bordewijk and van Kaam describe as 'registration'. This refers to the remote monitoring, information capture and data mining capabilities of communication systems that are essential, in the first instance, to bill for services and collect receipts. Registration systems harvest information from consumers rather than issue them with it. Programmatic control over the collection of information resides with the registration database, not the consumer. This type of interactivity is extremely important to new media environments because it can generate incredibly rich systemic feedback in the form of data that can be used for a wide variety of purposes, including personalizing interaction. The growth of registration is a major factor in the considerable resurgence of direct marketing in recent decades. The varieties of ways in which registration data can be used are discussed in Chapter 5.

As Bordewijk and van Kaam also acknowledge, most communication services and networks actually exhibit multiple patterns of information flow and interaction. The allocutionary features of agenda-setting newspapers are often more prominent than their consultation features, especially when compared to magazines that are usually targeted to narrower niche markets. Telecommunications networks rely on registration and conversation, and multichannel television systems principally deploy a mix of consultation and registration. In digital networked media, such as the internet, programmatic control is highly malleable. It can be dynamically deployed to support all types of interactivity. Control over programmability can also be distributed and networked. Digital, networked communications media such as the internet and cell phones can be programmed to support multi-patterned flows of information and a dynamic mix of types of interaction. This dynamic, multi-patterned, interactivity includes explicit conversational capabilities that enable peer-to-peer exchange, direct participation and representation. This capacity for conversational interaction distinguishes the new media from modern mass media, and is crucial to understanding the breadth and depth of consumer interest in these new media.

Bordewijk and van Kaam's scheme has been influential in media and communication studies as a foundation for more detailed theoretical work on the human interface with communications technologies (for example, Jensen 1999; Downes and McMillan 2000; McMillan 2002; Meikle 2002; Van Dijk 2006). Importantly, there is general agreement that the cybernetic properties of communication systems do not in any way account for the cultural complexity of meaning or the social significance of mediated communication. Approaching the same problem of interactivity from the perspective of cultural studies, Henry Jenkins helpfully proposes 'participation' to differentiate the practices and protocols of communication in living cultures from the interactive affordances of engineered systems (Jenkins 2006: 133). Where interactivity is a property of non-human actors, participation is a characteristic of human actors. Interactivity describes the technical possibilities of communication in closed systems, while participation denotes the will to communicate in cultural and social contexts. Thus, conversation comprises at least the two interrelated dimensions of interaction and participation.

Mediated communication is inherently a collaborative and socially constitutive process involving both human and non-human actors. Yet the interactive capabilities of different communication systems have different consequences for social participation. The possibilities of participation in markets, media and consumer culture that conversational media facilitate are qualitatively different to those of allocutionary mass media. Users are able to blend conversation with other types of interactivity to further their own interests and those of their social networks, in and through direct participation. New media environments extend the possibilities of conversational interaction and participation, and generate new possibilities of consumer productivity. These possibilities encompass direct involvement in the selection and distribution of media content, the appropriation and transformation of media content to create new content, and the generation and circulation of original content. The productive potential of conversational interaction and participation, especially as it is routinely encountered in the World Wide Web, is a significant development.

Conversation is often associated in communication theory with interpersonal communication, and includes three main modes of monologue, dialogue and discussion (Burnett and Marshall 2003: 49). It is a highly dynamic form of communication involving complex activities of listening, reciprocal turn-taking and the negotiated management of control over conversation, which can involve many people in the case of discussion. Digital networked media introduce a new conversational mode, which has been described as the 'multilogue' (Shank, quoted in Burnett and Marshall 2003: 49). This increases the variety and scale of conversational modes of communication. Digital networked media also makes multilogues even more complex by enabling the routine incorporation of different temporal and spatial dimensions in conversation. These make it possible, for example, for a group of globally dispersed people to meet in real time in a 'chat' environment; or to share reading recommendations asynchronously, on Amazon.com.

As a type of interactivity, conversation is more open-ended than allocution, consultation or registration. It differs from other types of interactivity to the extent that it is not an end in itself, 'but a means to a creative end' (Meikle 2002: 32). As the Coke–Mentos case illustrates, participants in conversational interaction can deploy an extensive array of media literacies in these processes, which exceed the ordinary meaning of conversation. They stretch it to include the collaborative creation and circulation of very elaborate performances and media productions, and are not limited to texts, images or hyperlinks. In considering the growing expanse of conversation-based practices, Graham Meikle proposes 'intercreativity' to describe the social relations of these developments in conversational interaction (Meikle 2002: 32). This term draws on the vision of HTML and World Wide Web creator, Tim Berners-Lee, who proposed the Web as a medium for convivial intercreativity, not just interactivity. Meikle suggests that intercreativity can be used to differentiate the more complex forms of online creative collaboration. As Table 1.1 indicates, intercreativity is a useful way to differentiate the social relations of new media from earlier forms of conversational media. Arguably, it is in the practices of intercreative participation that we are seeing some of the most interesting and challenging developments associated with the new media of mass conversation.

In their survey of the World Wide Web as a cultural phenomenon, Richard Burnett and P. David Marshall identify the 'promise of production' as a key factor to understanding its success (Burnett and Marshall 2003: 75, 201). Marshall also argues that the 'will to produce' is 'a pervasive cultural phenomenon that is elemental to the appeal of new media and the cultures it has spawned' (Marshall 2004: 52). However, neither the 'promise of production' nor 'the will to produce' are exclusive to the Web. Rather, prior to the internet, the capacity for widespread and routine participation in cultural production was frustrated in quite specific ways by the politics, economics and social organization of mass media, as well as their control architectures. European culture and media critics have argued that the dominance of the transmission model in the twentieth century was a consequence of deliberate choices made by governments and capital, which sought to limit the participatory capacity of citizens to talk back and of consumers to be producers, by constituting them as audiences (Enzensberger 1974; Brecht 1979). These perspectives reflect the instrumental importance of allocution to the rise of European fascism and authoritarianism in the first part of the twentieth century. They also point to the immense political and economic investment concentrated in transmission as potent obstacles to diverse communication ecologies. Cultural studies have also highlighted the ways in which audiences constantly circumvent these constraints on interactivity and participation (Marshall 2004) and suggest that we should not be surprised by the speed at which mass markets for conversational media have developed. This is not to say that constraints on interaction and participation are absent from new media environments. Rather, they are different, and these difference are the means by which a 'new version of politics as much as a new version of shopping is emerging from the loose Web' (Burnett and Marshall 2003: 200).

Ivan Illich (1985) spoke of the human desire for 'tools for conviviality', which could be used by people to 'invest the world' with meaning. In the early 1970s Illich argued the need to invest in tools, technologies and techniques, 'which give each person who uses them the greatest opportunity to enrich the environment with the fruits of his or her vision' (21). Industrial tools, Illich argued, 'deny this possibility to those who use them and they allow their designers to determine the meaning and expectations of others' (21). In opposing convivial and industrial tools, Illich points to the fluidity of the technology/society relation. When extrapolated to mediated communication, Illich's analysis suggests that the extent to which a culture is shaped by its media and communication systems is strongly influenced by the ease with which these systems can be used for individual and collective expression. The internet is a highly convivial medium (Lim 2003) and consequently a major source of user-led innovation in the development of communication tools (Tuomi 2002) and consumer culture (Arvidsson 2006). Cell phones support anywhere, anytime conversation. Because they are proprietary networks, however, the possibilities of user-led innovation are far more constrained than those of the internet (Goggin and Spurgeon 2007).Where mass media have been crucially important in shaping mass markets and mass society, conversational media theoretically enhance the production of a multiplicity of new market and social relations.

For much of the twentieth century, transmission – allocution in Bordewijk and van Kaam's scheme – was the prevailing model of communication, not conviviality. Not only did it dominate in the development of mass media technologies and institutions but it also shaped the professional communication disciplines of advertising, journalism, marketing and public relations. The transmission view had the effect of naturalizing unequal interaction between senders and receivers as the commonsense view of communication (Carey 1992). It legitimized restrictions on participation to those occasions where media gatekeepers elected to augment transmission and consultation with, for example, letters to the editor, talkback radio or popular voting in television shows. It also legitimated the concentration of the systemic and social power of communication in the sender, presupposing a high degree of certainty, if not rigidity, in wider social relations whereby, 'producers produce and communicate, while consumers receive and consume' (Varey 2002: 20).

The correspondence between Coca Cola's initial response to the Coke–Mentos experiments and the transmission view of communication was sharply noted in a number of marketing blogs.[2] Coke brand managers did not initially consider the quirkiness of the consumer-generated Coke–Mentos images to be well-aligned to the Coke brand personality. One brand manager was reported in the *Wall Street Journal* as having said that she preferred to think that consumers would do what Coke intended and drink the product rather than perform experiments with it (Vranica and Terhune 2006). The contrast with the more nimble, any-publicity-is-good-publicity response of Mentos was striking. Mentos was praised in online marketing networks for responding so favourably to its capture by the public imagination.

The implications of interactivity in media and communications systems are not easily fathomed when considered in isolation from the social practices of participation. The disjunction that arises between communication conceived in de-contextualized systemic terms, and communication conceived in terms of culture, becomes even more pronounced as conversational media technologies become ubiquitous. Conversational media confirm the passive receiver of mass media to be as much a fiction as the compliant consumer of mass markets. They erode the 'dialectical dichotomy of production and consumption' and the 'hierarchical structure' of communication senders and receivers (Marshall 2004: 103). Despite its incongruity with conversational media, the transmission view of communication is proving hard to shake. Richard Varey observes that 'marketing thinking and practice has not more generally adopted the participatory conception of communication' (Varey 2002: 75). He provides one of the few managerial accounts of marketing which views communication 'as inherently collaborative and cooperative visible behavior, rather than as merely personal cognition' (24) and argues that conversation, not transmission, is the core mode of communication in markets and society. Because mass media producers, distributors, marketers and communication professionals, including advertising agencies, 'want to maintain their traditional dominance over media content' (Jenkins 2003: 286) they struggle with the social implications of participation that accompany the rise of conversation-driven media and communications at the opening of the twenty-first century.

The social consequences and implications of conversational interactivity, especially intercreativity, are far-reaching (Benkler 2006). For advertising and advertiser-funded media the impacts of mass conversation are also enormously varied. The disruptive effects of new media on agency services and structures, as well as incumbent 'main' media markets and revenues (so-called because they are the media from which advertising agencies have historically derived commissions) are a source of ongoing anxiety in the trade press. The conversational paradigm provides a foundation for new market opportunities in e-businesses and new commercial media, as the success stories of Amazon.com and Google illustrate. Despite the setback of the 2000–01 dotcom market crash, new media start-ups continue to enter the market in proliferating numbers. Many appear to strengthen the position of individuals in the 'conversational haggle' of the 'virtual agora' that is the internet, where flows of communication, commerce, culture and politics intersect (Burnett and Marshall 2003: 106).

Advertising and the commercialization of new conversational media

How, and whether, the internet should develop as a platform for commerce and advertising has itself been the focus of ongoing contention. The internet has been curiously resistant to certain types of commercialization but very open to others. The first widespread commercial internet activity was the creation of markets for the provision of services, which provided public access to the internet. Although the backbone links of the internet were private networks, they were also a publicly-funded research infrastructure. The 'acceptable use' policy regime introduced by the US National Science Foundation (NSF) in 1990 formalized a self-regulatory approach for internet resource management. This prohibited expressly commercial communication, but not for ideological reasons. The NSF was more concerned with limiting its exposure to the escalating communications infrastructure costs arising from increased demand for connectivity than it was with constraining commercial communication (Reid 1997: xxi). Internet engineers working with quasi-commercial Internet Service Providers (ISPs) from about 1993 provided the first commercial internet access services. They started developing dial-up solutions to extend internet connectivity beyond universities. Browsers became available as user-friendly interfaces to the internet and the World Wide Web shortly thereafter. They had the effect of significantly boosting demand for internet connectivity, accelerating the demand for public access to internet services, and providing the impetus for a privatized, commercial internet future. By 1995 the private networks of commercial ISPs were so extensive that the NSF withdrew from access provision.

Commercializing the provision of the transport layers of the internet was achieved with such speed that internet access quickly became a commodity. Commercial ISPs pursued a variety of branding strategies to differentiate their services from others in unevenly developing, but rapidly growing markets. Commercializing the content and application layers of the internet has proven to be far more challenging. The utility business model of metered fee-for-service did not have widespread appeal beyond access. Instead, the fortunes of many internet start-ups of the mid- to late 1990s were tied to the internet's perceived potential for highly targeted advertising and marketing. John Brown and Paul Duguid (2002) note the structural tensions inherent in many early business plans. They were predicated on the continuation of mass media modes of advertising. They assumed, 'the continuing existence of large companies shelling out very large sums to advertise on the Web. Yet those same business plans also champion(ed) the end of those same large companies and the availability of "perfect" information' (Brown and Duguid 2002: 247).

Early advertising-funded internet business plans were often based on simplistic expectations that consumers and advertisers alike would flock to the Web because it could somehow be used to overcome the mass media problems of unwanted advertising and clutter. The main consumer benefit of highly targeted advertising was presumed to be the attraction of content subsidized by advertising that was so personalized and relevant it would be part of the medium's draw. The benefits to advertisers were similarly perceived to include the extent to which the accountability and flexibility of the Web exceeded existing mass and niche media, and advertiser interest in the predominantly single, young, white, educated and employed early internet user-base. Some of these elements were certainly important to the success of search engines and new search media business models. In practical effect, neither internet users nor advertisers paid much attention to these boosterist arguments. Similarly, the early internet advertising forms of banners and pop-ups were not well regarded. Misplaced confidence in the income-earning potential of banner advertising was one of a number of critical factors that saw many internet start-ups fail when the market value of technology stocks collapsed in the so-called dotcom bust of 2000–01 (Flew 2005: 147).[3]

Early internet users proved to be enormously resistant to being packaged as consumers. The 'honest broker' role of registration system operators, who aimed to develop the consumer profiles necessary for highly targeted advertising and position themselves as intermediaries between advertisers and Web destinations (Reid 1997: 210ff.), did not win consumer acceptance. Advertisers were often unimpressed by the effectiveness of ads merely viewed on the Web, or associated rate cards based on Web page impressions, preferring instead the 'click-through' as the basic unit for buying Web advertising space. Furthermore, national advertisers were less interested in the Web as an alternative to direct marketing and more interested in using it to build brand equity through softer selling techniques. They quickly found that they could develop their own Web-based, rich media destinations. Jeans brand Levi's was one of the first global brands to pursue such a Web-based branded content strategy (Reid 1997: 235).

The established advertising industry was not a significant stakeholder in the early commercial period of the internet. This initially poor understanding of the medium has prompted speculation about whether the fortunes of advertising, understood as a knowledge system, are too closely tied to mass media and the transmission view of communication, and whether the modern agency structure can survive the transition to a more diverse media and communication ecology (Cappo 2003: 162; Jaffe 2003:106; Turow 1997). Attitudes to and aptitudes for new media are certainly critical to agency resilience. Yet, creative advertising agencies in particular tended to be comparatively late new media adopters (Lesley Brydon Interview, 11 November 2005). Various commentators identify the failure of the 'above-the-line' advertising industry to be early movers at 'the leading edge of technology adoption' (Daniels 1997: 116) in either creative production or communication, as an important contributing factor in the current crisis of advertising. It is also curious given the industry's highly socially networked character. Agencies are built on 'a type of creative organization which makes a virtue out of teamwork, networks and project management', and which is characteristically 'strongly commercial and highly personalized' (Davis and Scase 2000: 46). The distributed innovation culture of the internet should have been a natural fit for agencies. Andrew Jaffe (2003: 178) speculates that the sustained period of agency mergers and global agency consolidation throughout the 1980s and 1990s contributed to agencies' reluctance to be early internet adopters. Where a small number of global holding companies ultimately manage accounts for a similarly concentrated number of global advertising clients, the risk of conflict of interest is high. Client suspicion about the security and integrity of ICT-supported knowledge networks within advertising is likely to be considerable. The Coke–Mentos example is suggestive of the role that fear of losing control of the brand might also play in this mix. This is not to say that marketing communication professions and advertising services have failed to cross the digital threshold. The impact of database applications has been massive (see Chapter 5). Important conceptual developments have also arisen when marketing communication professionals have embraced new media.

Cluetrain Manifesto co-authors Rick Levine, Christopher Locke, Doc Searles and David Weinberger were in the first wave of new media marketers to grasp the significance of internet-enabled conversation. They recognized the internet as a particularly efficient means of communication that would empower those people, 'so long ignored, so long invisible, that . . . they're figuring out what to do with the internet much faster than government agencies, academic institutions, media conglomerates, and Fortune-class companies' (Locke 2000: 175). Sociological studies show that internet users are far more historically and culturally specific than this analysis admits (for example, Castells 2002). Although exhilarating in its challenges, the underlying *Cluetrain* claim – that only civilized forms of capital which are willing and able to act on the understanding that 'markets are conversations' (Levine *et al.* 2000: ix) will prosper in the rapidly developing network economy – was also inadequately problematized. Nevertheless, another important *Cluetrain* proposition – that workers and customers would lose no time in making up for the 'two-hundred-year-long industrial interruption of the human conversation . . . both inside companies and in the marketplace' (Weinberger 2000: 163) – is now daily borne out by numerous examples, including those discussed in this book.

This line of thinking within marketing communication about the implications of conversational media continues to develop. It has been schematically elaborated upon in the Web 2.0 approach to making conversational media commercially productive. Popularized by Tim O'Reilly (2005), Web 2.0 broadly differentiates those internet businesses that survived and prospered following the collapse in the market value of technology stocks in 2000, from those that did not (Web 1.0). Where Web 1.0 firms view the internet as a platform for publishing and selling, Web 2.0 firms, such as Amazon.com and Google, use it as a services interface. They understand the primary importance of developing Web services to facilitate advertiser and consumer participation and interaction. They have turned away from the mass media model and the associated 'push' techniques of advertising. Instead, Web 2.0 firms understand that consumers will seek out advertising when they need or want it, and have found ways to integrate advertising unobtrusively across the internet.

Web 2.0 firms also grasp the changed economies of scope and scale that the internet opened up. For example, the inventories of Web-based firms were no longer limited by the physical constraints of the shopfront. It is just as possible to operate in micro-markets as it is in mass markets. Furthermore, sales in micro-markets are now cumulatively more valuable than sales in mass markets. Advertisers and consumers alike can also tap consumer expertise and knowledge of markets, products and services. These Web 2.0 features have been popularized by *Wired* journalist Chris Anderson (2004) as 'the Long Tail' of the network economy (see Chapter 2).

Both the *Cluetrain* and Web 2.0 propositions are highly suggestive of new ways for thinking about how Web-based markets might be constituted, how the relations of new Web-based markets might be developed and maintained, and how these new markets might be, indeed are, perceived and used by many consumers and advertisers alike. Web 2.0 propositions also highlight the extent to which advertising and marketing communication is still hamstrung by ideas of transmission, and draw attention to the radically disruptive potential of conversational media. For these reasons, Web 2.0 is being debated with a great deal of seriousness in new media and communication studies.[4] Both *Cluetrain* and Web 2.0 can also be understood as the brand propositions of self-made marketing communication gurus in a highly competitive industry where research is the industry's own currency for market differentiation. The question for critical researchers is how to engage with this kind of branded research.

Critical responses

It is interesting to consider why Web 2.0 has not been immediately discounted in new media studies as a product of the 'unworthy discourse' of advertising and marketing communication (Cunningham 1992). Critical political economists of media and communications could be predicted to argue that this development is further evidence of the complicity of new media and cultural studies in the relentless colonization of social space and the commoditization of culture by capital (Graham 2006). Cultural studies critics might be predicted to counter with the claim that there needs to be a more nuanced, but no less critical, appreciation of the historical contribution that advertising and marketing communication disciplines have made to understanding the social specificity and complexity of consumption and markets.

Kathy Myers (1986) argued in her analysis of the major economic critiques of advertising made from both the left and right of the political spectrum over the last century, that advertising 'comes nearer to a research-based theory of consumption' than any other discipline (48). Modern economic thought, from which modern marketing sprang, has regarded consumption as a reaction to 'that which has already been produced' (130). However, one of the key discoveries of advertising has been that commodities and needs, like consumption, 'are social in origin' (131). The strength of advertising lies in the fact that it escapes the historical 'intellectual division of labour' (Slater 2002: 71) that plagues most academic approaches taken to advertising, consumption and markets. Ultimately, advertising seeks to integrate its economic and cultural roles, and the best advertising disregards this disciplinary compartmentalization. Advertising's success depends on its ability to match both these aspects of social life to the particular relations of production and consumption of concern at any given time.

Both critical political economy and cultural perspectives offer valuable insights on the problems of advertising and marketing communication, but a problem that many political economy critiques have not yet adequately addressed is the presumption that consumers are being systematically duped by advertising and its ideological influences on commercial media (Myers 1986: 204). New media studies tend to inherit from cultural studies the resistance to any presumption that media consumers are unknowing participants in communicative relationships with commercial media and advertisers. Critical traditions that proceed from an assumption that the social relations of mass communication in capitalist mass societies are inequitable and unfair, are not always helpful for navigating the surprising terrain of conversational media. While questions of media citizenship are a central theme of new media studies, the disruptive consequences of mass conversation for fixed notions of media consumption are also compelling. For these reasons, new media studies seem curious about the window of opportunity that marketing communication disciplines might open for applying critical insights to the imaginings and social shaping of economically viable, convivial, new media markets and citizen consumers. Identifying the limits to this coincidence of the interests in critical enquiry in new media, and professional marketing communication practices is, undoubtedly, an important challenge for new media studies. Rational self-interest in profit or material gain explains only a small proportion of consumption practices, including those encountered in conversational media, but it remains the core motivation of commercial enterprises.

Advertising and marketing communication industries and professions are subject to a wide range of other important economic and social constraints, including the limits of their own pragmatics. One area of indeterminacy in the marketing communication propositions epitomized by *Cluetrain* and Web 2.0 concerns the definition of commercial media in a new, conversational media context. Most discussions of new media tend to blur e-commerce and new commercial media. The line between e-commerce firms such as Amazon.com and eBay, and Web-based commercial media, such as the search media giant Google, is not always easily discerned. New commercial media enterprises can, theoretically, easily flip from being principally advertising-funded to being principally funded from other income sources, such as sales or commissions on sales. They can also draw income from subscriptions, but in the main do not because of consumer demand for 'free' contact and content services (Picard 2000).

Importantly, not all new commercial media fit the Web 2.0 mould. Mass and niche media are also adapting to the conversational challenge. If the new conversational media are truly convivial then the end of the 'radical monopoly' (Illich 1985: 52) of transmission is not likely to produce another radical monopoly of interaction in its place. Indeed, multichannel pay TV was an important expansion of consumer choice in consultation and registration-based media in North America and parts of Europe and predated the World Wide Web. These services also introduced a new subscriber-funded business model. To the extent that they were not reliant on advertising, and in many cases did not carry it, they were the first new media services that 'broke the mould of the broadcast model in both its traditional public and private forms' (Sinclair 2004: 43).

Firms such as Google, Yahoo!, YouTube, Revver and the numerous other advertising-funded Web 2.0 media, mobilize highly malleable ideas of advertisers, consumers and media producers. As the Coke–Mentos example illustrates, these media enterprises service the possibility that consumers can be advertisers and media producers; that advertisers can be media producers and consumers; and that media producers are also advertisers and consumers. The implications of new media for subjectivity have also been framed by active theories of media audiences. New media consumers have been variously theorized as the citizen consumers

(Hartley 2005: 9ff.) of participatory DIY media cultures (Jenkins 2003: 287); as the 'prosumers' (Toffler 1970) of participatory fan cultures (Marshall 2004: 25; Jenkins 2006); as 'viewsers' (O'Regan and Goldsmith 2002: 103), 'co-creators' (Banks 2002) and 'productive players' (Humphreys 2005) of computer games; and as the 'produsers' of networked social software such as blogs (Bruns and Jacobs 2006). The creative agency of consumers has been understood by marketing since the mid-1950s (Packard 1960: 70ff.; Arvidsson 2006). Adam Arvidsson argues that this agency has been 'enhanced by the process of mediatization of consumption, and in particular through the impact of electronic media' which strengthens the productive capacity of interaction and social participation (Arvidsson 2006: 14). This capacity is now fundamentally reshaping the social relations of commercial media.

A history of co-adaptation

This book considers the adaptation of the advertising-funded business model in new media contexts and pays particular attention to the limits and opportunities for citizen consumers to renegotiate the terms of advertising and consumption in new commercial media environments. Also of interest is the way that advertising and commercial media industries are co-adapting in order to remain relevant to the consumers that are desirable to advertisers.

The process of co-adaptation is continuous, as the trend in professional communication theory and practice to 'through-the-line' (Berry 1998) or Integrated Marketing Communication (IMC) illustrates. In the past two decades, this broad development has provided important accounts for why advertising is being decentred as the pre-eminent marketing communication discipline. In the IMC approach, advertising is regarded as one tool in a marketing communication kit that also includes public relations, direct selling, customer relationship management and other forms of promotion. Ideally, IMC seamlessly unifies internal and external communication strategies, and ensures consistent representation of an advertiser's organizational and market identity (Schulz 1999). In its more commonplace practices, IMC is concerned with finding ways 'under the radar' of consumers who are indifferent or resistant to advertising (Bond and Kirshenbawm 1998).

IMC is an important response to the globalization of markets and technological change (Cappo 2003; McAllister 1996: 7; Schulz 1999). Consumer societies continue to emerge around the world. Mature consumer economies also continue to experience growth, notably in the globalizing services sectors, which support the multinational coordination of capital. Media, communications, information and entertainment platforms and services have multiplied, diversified and globalized. Audiences, readerships and markets have simultaneously fragmented, sometimes into niches that can be globally exploited, even though they are more challenging for advertisers to reach. Many advertisers have consequently reconsidered their mass media advertising strategies and now seek to augment, complement or integrate a greater diversity of highly targeted media and promotional tactics into their communication strategies in order to optimize opportunities to communicate with consumers. Advertising now exhibits 'a highly dichotomized structure comprising a small number of larger firms with an international orientation' which have expanded horizontally into other marketing communication specializations, and large numbers of small firms with a primarily local (national) orientation' (Daniels 1997: 109). It has also bifurcated along media buying and creative specializations (Davis and Scase 2000: 45) which are either owned by global agency networks or much smaller privately-owned enterprises (Nixon 2003: 136; Sinclair 2006, 116). The trend to global consolidation and integration of marketers, markets and marketing communication also has its counter-trends. The relatively slow response of internationally-oriented agencies to new media has seen the emergence of small, fast-moving, media-neutral and new media-savvy, strategic and creative specialists who have proven to be highly competitive with their established agency network counterparts. Specialist new media marketing services continue to emerge, for example in search optimization and mobile marketing. Innovation also continues to occur in integrated marketing communication strategies and new media advertising techniques.

The touchpoint marketing framework is one example of how IMC informs a new mode 'of consumer–advertiser interaction that is increasingly individuated, privatized and directed away from the public domain of mass communication' (Malefyt 2006: 95). Advertising and media partners collaborate to create multiple points of contact with consumers in a product consumption cycle as marketing communication opportunities. The focus is on the interrelationship of the experience of consumption with the emotional state of consumers. It seeks to tap the 'affective' economy of the senses and feelings (Jenkins 2006: 20). Fast food brands often provide good illustrations of integrated touchpoint marketing practices and the use of affective economics in marketing communication (Malefyt 2006). New personalized entertainment media and communication technologies lend themselves to these strategies, and using them can give advertisers some confidence of reaching consumers while minimizing their exposure in mass media and to public rejection. While touchpoint marketing might address the perceived problems of mass media for control of brand identity, it is not at all clear that it is an effective brand prophylactic in conversational modes of public opinion formation.

Co-adaptation is continuous, but it can also be an acrimonious affair. Just as civic interests in media have vied for the upper hand in the design and allocation of media resources (Smulyan 1994), advertisers and commercial mass media share a history of rivalries and power struggles for supremacy especially in matters such as costs, agency remuneration and editorial control of media content. Various commercial media histories note the ways in which advertises have worked 'to shape the media to their needs' (Turow 1997: 162). Advertiser relations with pre-television commercial radio, for example, were often qualitatively different to those of the press. National advertisers accumulated extensive influence in radio programming through programme supply and sponsorship arrangements (Fox 1997), whereas access to newspapers was generally on terms and conditions dictated by editors and proprietors (McFall 2004). With the arrival of broadcast television, media owners successfully broke the nexus of advertiser control over content by moving to a business model that was based on the sale of interstitial airtime, or spots (Turner 2004: 14). The balance of power once again began to tip back towards advertisers with the expansion of broadcasting services to include niche and multichannel services (McAllister 1996: 28; Leiss *et al.* 2005). The regulatory environment was also a factor in this rebalancing of media and advertiser power relations. In Europe, North America and elsewhere, the accreditation arrangements that had been developed in the first part of the century by media proprietors, and which enabled them to control agency entry into media sales and lucrative commission income, were brought to an end in the latter part of the century (Cappo 2003: 31; Mattelart 2002: 20; Ogilvy 2004: 109ff.).

There are important exceptions to this historical sweep of advertising and commercial media relations in the twentieth century. Organized consumer movements, now active in most parts of the world, have played vital local, national and international roles in consumer rights advocacy. Their activities have often addressed misleading, deceptive and unethical advertising practices, but they also take in a much broader range of concerns. On occasions, the campaigns mounted by these organizations have delivered decisive victories to consumer interests in the structure and regulation of markets, and for this they are reviled by free market purists (for example, Hood 2005). In the main, however, individual media consumers have been sidelined in the struggles between commercial media organizations and their commercial clients. Structurally positioned as receivers of communication, and as commodities to be sold by media owners back to advertisers, the social influence of individual mass media consumers was highly constrained when compared to the tactical influence that new media consumers can now exert.

Ultimately, though, it is not necessary to establish whether the examples such as the EepyBird Coke–Mentos experiments are tactical interventions that poke fun at the brands and their products or whether they are calculated efforts on the part of amateur performance artists to turn professional, or both. This case illustrates the larger point of particular interest here: that the creative participation of individual consumers and bottom-up processes of consumer self-organization are being realized in conversational media. Furthermore, this development is deeply implicated in the social shaping and re-shaping of advertising-funded media.

Advertising and new media

Anne Cronin (2004) makes a useful distinction between academic work that is broadly directed to the question, 'how does advertising work?' and that which asks, 'what is the work of advertising?' (Cronin 2004: 113). The first question characterizes the historical body of positivist scholarship, which generally forms the core business of the professional communication disciplines of advertising and marketing communication. The second question characterizes the wider range of concerns about advertising and commercial media that are often critically framed in other knowledge domains. These domains include, but are certainly not limited to, media studies, cultural studies, consumption studies, as well as media anthropology, sociology, politics and political economy. Martin Davidson (1992) observes that this openness of advertising studies comes about because advertising's use of 'language and image, of social values and cultural archetypes, goes far beyond the boundaries of the product itself' (6). Cronin's demarcation is polemical and therefore does not seek to accommodate the extent to which these two broad approaches to advertising are mutually informing or constitutive. Many innovations in advertising practice have been attributed to interdisciplinary appropriation and decontextualization of critical methods and approaches, which in turn has provoked a degree of interdisciplinary tension (Davidson 1992: 196; Mattelart 2002: 147–70; 200ff.; Frank 1997; Mort 1996: 103; Quart 2003: 12, 57).

This book traverses aspects of the first question about how advertising works in the course of seeking to understand the work that advertising does in conversational media. It is concerned with the disruptive social influence of intercreative participation on the advertising-funded media business model as well as the political economy of commercial conversational media. It is organized around key, recurrent themes in professional and critical discourses of advertising. Chapter 2 contrasts two major contemporary trends in the ongoing co-adaptation of advertising and media. It relates developments in conversational media to the rapid rise of internet search engines and their transition to highly influential search media (Battelle 2005). It identifies search culture as one of the most important influences on innovations in informational and creative approaches to advertising. These approaches are linked, in turn, to broad historical trends in advertising, and related debates about the social role and value of advertising. As Armand Mattelart (2002: 204) explains, since the 1930s a distinction has been drawn between 'good and bad advertising; between informative advertising and the advertising of persuasion and manipulation'. The new search media such as Google rely on interesting and important developments in informational advertising techniques that are enabled by networked ICTs and conversational interaction. Like classifieds, they can be aligned to inherited norms of 'good' informational advertising. Branded content, which can include anything from product placement to advertiser-funded entertainment, represents a similarly interesting and important range of developments in corporate persuasive advertising and marketing techniques. These techniques are often the focus of influential critiques of advertising (for example, Klein 2000). While the informational and creative/persuasive distinction continues to be useful as a typology of advertising techniques, it is argued in Chapter 2 that its usefulness as a hierarchy of the social value of advertising is seriously constrained in new, advertising-funded media contexts. Developments in informational as well as creative and persuasive approaches have major implications for future possibilities of disinterested media content and communication tools.

Another normative hierarchy of value is associated with different kinds of interpersonal and mediated conversations. This accords high social status to those forms deemed artful, rational, instrumental or goal-directed. As feminist research into telephone usage has shown, intrinsic forms of conversation, including gossip, are crucial to the development and maintenance of social networks, irrespective of their particular functions or purposes (Spender 1995; Van Zoonen 2002; Rakow 1997). Other developments that have precipitated a re-evaluation of the role of hitherto low-status forms of conversation include cultural studies of media celebrity. This work calls attention to the ease with which critical media studies has tended to discount communication that does not support rational conversation (Turner, Bonner and Marshall 2000: 15). Marketers have always accorded a high value to intrinsic kinds of conversation such as gossip. They value personal selling as the most effective marketing communication technique, and prize consumer word-of-mouth as the most highly effective of all (Blackshaw and Nazzaro 2004; Searles 2000: 83). Intrinsic conversations, it turns out, are not necessarily commercial-free zones. Furthermore, conversational media facilitate the spread of ideas at astonishing speed through dispersed social networks (Rushkoff 1994; Gladwell 2002), as the Coke–Mentos case illustrates. The importance of intrinsic conversation to creative productivity is also recognized as a notable feature of creative and cultural industries (especially advertising), if not the wider economy (Davis and Scase 2000). In many respects, new conversational media intensifies commercial reliance on a feminized mode of communication. Yet, as Chapter 3 shows, this contrasts starkly with many advertising industry norms, including the gendering of creativity as a masculine attribute in creative advertising practice.

This book pays critical attention to the claim that, at the opening of the new millennium, individual users have emerged as significant actors to be reckoned with in the power plays of new media and communications. It offers a number of important qualifications in the course of attending to the relations of advertising and media in selected contemporary, geopolitical and social contexts. Chapter 4, for example, turns to the case of the People's Republic of China to consider the role of advertising in the development of mass markets for cellular telephone services. Viewed on a global scale, the barriers to internet access mean that it has developed, and continues to develop, as a communications infrastructure of relative privilege. The picture is somewhat more complex for cell phones where adoption rates have had quite dramatic effects on teledensity rates in many countries (ITU 2002). Internet and internet-like services are also accessible via cell phone services in many parts of the world, but the terms and conditions of access can be quite different to those of the PC-accessed internet. A variety of influences have a bearing on these differences, including the fact that these services are most commonly proprietary value added services, and have often been developed in the first instance as branding strategies for telecommunications companies or handset manufacturers. How the cell phone might be made to work as an advertising platform is also under active consideration (see Chapters 4 and 5).

There are many major contemporary debates concerning advertising regulation. Chapter 5 focuses on the regulatory debates emerging around questions of information management and control. New media such as the internet and cell phones are not just important technologies of mass conversation. They are also direct response advertising media because they are transaction as well as communication channels. They support the means for harvesting end-user data in previously unimaginable detail and amounts. These kinds of remote monitoring applications are features of the type of interactivity that Bordewijk and van Kaam described as 'registration'. Understanding registration is crucially important to understanding the selling power of new conversational media and the new media businesses of mass conversation. Registration augments conversation, and often substitutes for it. It is the means by which new media and e-commerce destinations 'remember' consumers and customize subsequent visits. It enhances the 'stickiness' of new media. The consequences of on-selling data to third party direct marketing and market research specialists can be more problematic, especially where it is not anonymized. This chapter draws on mobile marketing and spam examples to illustrate the regulatory challenges of registration.

As competition for advertising income has intensified between growing numbers of advertising-dependent media enterprises, the risk for commercial media is that advertising shifts from a sellers' to a buyers' market. The catch for advertisers is that they often find they need to spend more on advertising in order to reach the same proportions of consumers in fragmented media markets as they did through mass media. As media markets fragment, mass media advertising revenues have been placed under increasing pressure. Although there are important local variations in the advertising markets of mature and emerging consumer societies, new media generally stimulate the overall amount spent on advertising and so it continues to grow in real terms as it has with the introduction of all new media throughout the twentieth century (Picard 2002). The proportion of revenue being captured by different media is changing in line with the media choices of consumers, especially those with high disposable incomes who are particularly sought after by advertisers. These shifts have significant consequences for media content and advertising techniques. While advertorials, infomercials, product placement and branded content are not new advertising techniques (Galician 2004), they are flourishing in the expanding, conversational media, communications and entertainment environment. How incumbent mass and niche media respond to the rise of conversational media is important in any account of advertising and new media. Chapter 6 concludes this study of advertising and new media by considering the adaptive strategies of commercial media incumbents. The incentives for media and entertainment conglomerates, old and new, to position themselves as integrated marketing agents in their own right, are strong. However, new media enterprises have a potentially significant advantage over incumbent conglomerates in this scenario. Paying particular attention to News Corporation, Chapter 6 explores the structural tension that businesses built on the exclusive exploitation of cultural commodities encounter in a world where non-exclusive trade in information is the ascendant norm of commerce and consumer culture.

Chapter 2

From the 'Long Tail' to 'Madison and Vine'

Trends in advertising and new media

Media economists, advertising industry practitioners and their critics have long distinguished between informational advertising and other forms that rely on so-called creative techniques of persuasion or direct comparison (Mattelart 2002: 204; Myers 1986: 147; Turner 1965: 9–11; Ogilvy 2004: 179–81; Hood 2005; Luhmann 2000; Schudson 1993). Because it appeals to reason and usually addresses the fulfilment of human needs, many advertising critics have reluctantly conceded that informational advertising is economically and socially beneficial. Creative and persuasive techniques have received less favourable consideration because they seek to influence purchasing decisions by indulging human emotions and wants, and rely on fabricating difference where it might not otherwise be found. Similarly, direct comparison is often considered to be a poor advertising practice but, like other types of creative and persuasive advertising, it tends to be both legal and effective.

This dichotomization of advertising techniques and their associated social benefits is problematic for many reasons. It betrays a prejudice that favours print cultures over the popular visual cultures in which creative advertising techniques have thrived (Jhally 2002). It also assumes that advertisers predetermine the symbolic and use values which consumers assign to goods and services, and that these values are fixed in advertising and marketing processes. In other words, the judgement that the rational appeal is the lesser of the two evils of advertising is anchored by the assumption that consumers and media audiences are passive, and that perfect information in a market can really only be attained through rational, instrumental allocution. Arguing against this view of advertising, Kathy Myers observes that the real 'crime' of creative and persuasive advertising,

> is not its ability to play on people's desires and fantasies. Arguably art, literature and culture also do that. Rather, it is the subtle substitution of an object for a dissatisfaction. Consumption becomes a displacement and a solution. The image is pleasurable in its own right, not an incentive to action, but rather an alternative to it.
>
> (Myers 1986: 140)

The problems of using the distinction between informational and creative and persuasive advertising as a normative guide to the social value of advertising are even more pronounced in new conversational media contexts. As the Coke–Mentos case considered in Chapter 1 clearly illustrates, consumers actively participate in negotiating the symbolic and use values of goods and services. The distinction is nonetheless a useful typology of advertising techniques. It is used here to frame a discussion of the two major contemporary trends in advertising. The aim is to better understand how informational and creative and persuasive approaches are changed by the influence of conversational interaction and social participation, and to consider the implications of these developments for commercial media.

The internet search engine is, perhaps, the single most important development for informational advertising since the time of the first paid newspaper advertisements or the telephone directory. In less than a decade, search engines have transformed into new, globally significant and, increasingly, locally relevant, advertising-funded media services and institutions (Battelle 2005). In the first instance, these new media make Web-based information highly discoverable. Search-based advertising confirms the importance of the informational value of advertising, but it also confounds the social relations of advertising. Citizen consumers use search media to target useful information. They self-select qualifying results, which may include a mix of Web-based advertising, tales of personal experience and opinion, gossip, testimonials, editorial comment or a more dispassionate evaluation. Search advertisers target search terms rather than consumers. Search media also extend the availability of advertising services to small advertisers who mainly rely on informational approaches to advertising and who have been neglected or taken for granted by mass media for a long time. Search culture is, fundamentally, based on conversational interaction and social participation, and it is booming. This is reflected in not only the extraordinary success of search media but also in broader changes in informational advertising, including the rapid movement online of classified and directory advertising. Search culture is also having a direct impact on creative and persuasive advertising approaches and techniques.

Online advertising expenditure now frequently exceeds outdoor, cinema and magazine advertising expenditure, and rivals radio advertising expenditures in many countries (ZenithOptimedia 2006). In the UK, internet advertising expenditures surpassed those for radio in 2006 (IAB UK 2006). Display advertising, search advertising and classified advertising are the three main types of online advertising. Display advertising attracted many advertisers to the internet in the 1990s, but also drove them away when it could not be established that banner advertising was particularly effective. Advertising in search engines and online directories is the largest, and one of the fastest growing segments of online advertising. It has financed the rapid emergence of search engines as highly influential new commercial media

(Battelle 2005). Search-based advertising in social networks is also growing at extraordinary rates (eMarketer 2007), a development reflected in the corporate strategies of 'old' and 'new' media companies alike. In 2006 Google agreed to pay $US900 million for exclusive rights to provide search and text-based search advertising on the hugely popular social network MySpace and other Fox Network online properties (van Duyn and Waters 2006). This was followed soon after by Google's other major move into linking search to social networks in 2006: the acquisition of YouTube for $US1.65 billion worth of Google stock (Google 2006). Rupert Murdoch's News Corporation had previously acquired MySpace in 2005 in a deal worth $US580 million.

In 2005 online advertising's share of total advertising expenditure in the USA was just under 5 per cent (PWC 2006). In the UK it reached 10 per cent in 2006 (IAB UK 2006). While this may seem small relative to the accompanying new media industry hype, the rates of growth for online advertising's share of total expenditures are extremely high. In the USA, online advertising grew by 33 per cent between 2004 and 2005. In the same period it grew by 40 per cent in the UK, and 60 per cent in Australia (ABVS 2005). It is these growth rates that boost the value of new media properties, and which make 'old' media proprietors nervous.

This chapter considers the distinctive historical market positions of three search media – Yahoo!, Google and Sensis. Yahoo! and Google are highly recognizable global search media brands. Sensis, on the other hand, is a national Australian brand owned by the dominant Australian telecommunications carrier. The contrasts between the business strategies of these global and national search media point to the variety of institutional and organizational cultures that vie for influence in the new search media: from the sensibilities of Hollywood to the techno-meritocratic, hacker cultures of the internet (Castells 2002) to telecommunications goliaths.

Interest in classified advertising, historically a very important form of informational advertising, has also been renewed due to the development of search culture and search media. The rapid migration of his type of advertising from print to online media has been powerfully driven by the increased control that online, search-based publication extends to end-users over many aspects of daily life, including the ways that people look for work, a home, transport and love. The growth in online, classified advertising also shows that these 'rivers of gold' are much longer and more varied than ever imagined by modern newspapers, the first home of classified advertising.

New search media, online directories and classifieds have led the charge to optimize the informational value of predominantly small advertisers to end-users. Indeed, small advertisers are largely responsible for the recovery of online advertising. They form an important part of what *Wired Magazine* editor, Chris Anderson, has called the 'Long Tail' of the digital economy (Anderson 2004). This term describes the demand dynamics of networked, informational economies that distinguish Web 2.0 media and e-commerce firms from industrial mass and niche media and markets. In mass media markets, a comparatively small number of media outlets have a mass consumer base. The demand curve for these media is small but steep. This, it turns out, continues to be the case for digital networked media. The important difference is, however, that many more Web-based media can be viably produced for much smaller audiences. The economics of new networked media support a demand curve that has both a steep head and a long shallow tail of demand. Most significant is the realization that the tail of the demand curve can be cumulatively more valuable to advertisers than the head.

While search culture makes small advertisers more discoverable, big advertisers are exploring the creative potential of proliferating channels, networked devices and increasingly abundant bandwidth to reach and engage the consumers of most value to them. National advertisers and global brands are the main proponents of creative advertising. They are compelled to develop innovative marketing communication strategies, not only by the proliferation of media and entertainment choices but also by the increasing ubiquity of search in all forms of electronic media. As John Battelle observes in his insightful study of search media, electronic programme guides and personal video recorders are navigation interfaces.

> What is TiVo, after all, but a search interface for television? iTunes? Search for music.
>
> (Battelle 2005: 253)

Many large national and transnational advertisers are dissatisfied with the uncertain performance of 'old' media. They are looking for new ways to reach increasingly distracted, distrustful and disinterested consumers. In order to avoid being a cause of irritation and interruption, many of these advertisers creatively embed their messages in media flows and experiences that coveted consumers will actively seek out. This is the trend to branded content. It is helpfully thought of as a continuum of creative advertising possibilities, with product placement, advertorial and infotainment located at one end, and full-blown content production at the other. In recent years, there has been an increase of advertiser activity at the content production end, with advertisers directly engaging in content production. Investments at this end of the branded content spectrum can be far more substantial than for those of the infomercial or advertorial, forms that emerged with the home shopping channels on cable television and in the suburban press. Movies, podcasts, games and live events, all with high production values, are being funded in the convergence of advertising and entertainment industries. So too are online destinations, many with outstanding interactive functionality, which aim to support branded online communities and social networks. This particular trend in branded content has been described as a meeting of 'Madison and Vine', a reference to the respective historical centres of the internationalized American advertising and entertainment industries on Madison Avenue in New York and Vine Street in Hollywood (Donaton 2004).

The Long Tail of new, networked media markets is a major development for an informational approach to advertising, just as the convergence of Madison and Vine is for creative approaches. Both trends have had important impacts on commercial media. They have contributed to rapid changes in the types of advertisers attracted to newspapers and commercial television, as well as the ways in which they use these media. They have also stimulated rapid growth in new, online, commercial media and entertainment forms.

This analysis begins to map the extent to which trends in informational and creative advertising destabilize incumbent mass and niche media markets and businesses. These developments also expand and increase the dynamism of the analytical category of media. While reliance on advertising revenues is an important indicator, many of the examples presented here also highlight the ease of movement that is possible between e-commerce and advertising business models, and the importance of an approach to understanding the new commercial media that permits this fluidity.

We are all advertisers now? Informational search and advertising's 'Long Tail'

Yahoo! was one of the earliest new media companies to turn profitable when, in 1998, it reported an $US18 million profit on a $US245 million turnover that had been generated substantially from advertising (Yahoo! 2000). Established in 1994 and publicly listed in 1996, Yahoo! aimed to help integrate the internet into daily life by providing an online destination where people would find all they needed or were looking for. In contrast to its main competitor, AOL, Yahoo! was not a proprietary network or internet service provider. It provided a range of communications services to consumers, such as email, in exchange for registration information that could be used for a range of purposes, including demonstrating the effectiveness of search as an advertising medium. Like AOL, Yahoo! had the look and feel of an internet portal. Although it started out as a series of curated lists and service directories, it quickly developed as one of the first new commercial search media, so-called after the search engine functionality at its heart (Battelle 2005). Search automated the conversational structure of end-user interaction with Yahoo! By December 1997 Yahoo! was recording 65 million page impressions per day from 20 million unique monthly visitors (Yahoo! 1997). Registration functionality embedded in search meant that Yahoo! could account to advertisers at levels of detail that were unprecedented in mass media. This excited advertiser interest in the potential of the internet as an advertising medium.

However, Yahoo! advertising revenues suffered significantly following the collapse of internet stock market values in April 2000. Many Yahoo! advertisers at that time were themselves internet-related companies and Yahoo! experienced a sudden contraction when many failed. Yahoo!'s own share price collapsed, even though site traffic volumes continued to grow. By the end of 2000 Yahoo! claimed 180 million unique visitors worldwide and 900 million average daily page impressions (Yahoo! 2000). One of the worst global slumps in advertising in 2002, felt throughout the advertising and commercial media industries, slowed recovery for Yahoo! A complicating factor for new media in this period was the lack of coherent industry standards for assessing the performance of online media. Related to this was the questionable effectiveness of, and levels of end-user resistance to, the early dominant forms of online advertising, notably the banner ad and the pop-up.

In 2001 former Warner Brothers chief executive Terry Semel took over day-to-day management. Yahoo! relocated to Hollywood and repositioned itself as a media and entertainment company in an attempt to diversify income sources. The company perceived itself to be over-reliant on advertising revenues. By 2004 Yahoo! was turning over $US3.6 billion, more than double its 2003 revenues (Yahoo! 2004). Yahoo!'s income comes from two distinct sources. Marketing services account for the lion's share of Yahoo! revenues and include activities such as keyword advertising on Yahoo! websites as well as affiliate sales network sites. A comparatively small amount comes from subscriptions and fees for premium rate content and communication services.

More than 8 million people paid for Yahoo!-branded premium services in 2004. Although the revenues for premium services are small compared to the core business of advertising, Yahoo! is investing heavily in developing this part of its business. It is building its profile as a search-based entertainment portal in anticipation of the imminent arrival of broadband internet in living rooms across the globe. In August 2005 Yahoo! had 388 million monthly registered users worldwide, nearly three-quarters of whom were broadband users. Over 24 million of these users streamed more than 2.9 billion videos in 2004 and spent more than 3 hours per week with Yahoo! in the process. Yahoo!'s stated aim is to increase this to 4 or 5 hours per week, to extend the social networks it supports in the process and to become the leading lifestyle and entertainment community portal. It has a major commitment to the digitization of video archives. It regularly adds new extensions such as Yahoo! Photos, which make it easy to share consumer-generated multimedia content – from photos to videos – on a cross-media basis. It has developed enhanced video, music, blog and podcasting media search functionality and moved into mobile content aggregation and dissemination. Although it aspires to be much more than a multi-platform, advertising-funded media services provider, growth in the premium content side of the Yahoo! business still has a very long way to go before this ambition is realized.

Google is another of the new search media which now shares with modern commercial media a business model that relies on advertising as its principle revenue source. Google raised $US23 billion when it made its initial public offering (IPO) in August 2004. Less than a year later, Google was valued at $US81 billion. This exceeded the listed value of older media and entertainment corporations, including Time Warner, which have arguably accumulated far more substantial assets than the new media upstart. The 2004 market appraisal of Google did not necessarily signal a return to the overheating of new media stock of the 2000 dotcom bust. Instead, Google's market value also reflects renewed advertiser confidence in internet advertising, and the search media business model in particular. In the few short years since its establishment, Google has grown rapidly to become a globally recognized brand. The technical sophistication of Google search products, which produce outstanding search results, remains a key factor in explaining Google's popularity with end-users and advertisers alike. The widespread popularity of Google search is reflected in the incorporation of the brand name into the lexicon of popular digital culture as a verb to describe the act of internet-based searching.

While Yahoo! is evolving as a search-based entertainment portal, Google retains a sharp, information technology focus. Google believes that search product development is the core of its competitive advantage among search media. Google had initially tried, unsuccessfully, to remain at arm's length from advertising by licensing its unique Web search technology to third parties. However, it quickly found that advertising more reliably delivered the revenues it needed for growth. The early Google concern for a public service orientation to search, untainted by commercial interests, is still apparent in numerous features, including its clutter-free, informational search and results interface, which is a markedly different design approach to the portal. End-user perceptions of Google as an accurate, reliable and comprehensive information source are also shaped by Google's corporate commitment to 'do no evil'. For these reasons, John Battelle portrays Google as a reluctant media company, at times torn between the *laissez faire* ideals of early internet culture and Web 2.0 rhetoric on the one hand and the corporate realities of running a global business on the other (Battelle 2005).

Google now generates income from a number of advertising and marketing services. Prominent among these is the sale of advertising space (known as inventory in advertising parlance) adjacent to search results. The method Google uses for pricing and selling inventory is the keyword auction. Advertisers, or their agents, bid for their positions on Google websites, as well as those of Google partners and sales network affiliates, in a real time, Web-based, auction market-place. The auction mechanism differentiates market values for keywords. Consequently, the costs for placing advertising adjacent to search results for a term such as 'home loan' are much higher than more obscure keywords for which there may be little or no competition. By 2001, a year after it had started auctioning keywords to advertisers, 77 per cent of Google's income came from advertising services. In 2002 that proportion had risen to 94 per cent and by 2004 it accounted for 98 per cent of Google's $US1.3 billion revenues in the first six months of that year (Google 2004).

The auction system of marketing advertising inventory was first developed by internet start-up Overture, now wholly owned by Yahoo! This approach allowed advertisers to optimize access to highly desirable, self-selecting market segments by dynamically contextualizing the placement of advertising messages in relevant search results. The audience unit of measure initially sold by the Overture auction system was the page impression, priced on a 'cost per thousand' (cpm) basis. When Google followed Overture's lead into keyword auctioning with the launch of AdSense it introduced an important variation and offered 'pay-per-click' as a basic unit of measure. This meant that advertisers paid only for self-selecting click-throughs, also referred to as 'qualified leads', because they are considered more likely to proceed to a transaction than the broader population of search users. The Google approach was initially well received by advertisers as a more precise indicator of return on their advertising investment. Google has since begun to extend its media brokerage services to other media (Kalehoff 2005), and triggered industry speculation about whether the auction might eventually be adopted as the basis for determining advertising rates across all media, replacing the more arbitrary mass media practices of setting rate cards. In this way, the auction mechanism has opened up the promise of completely revolutionizing the approach to pricing advertising inventory for all media as well as the social relations of advertising-funded media. Such a system would optimize advertiser access to highly desirable, self-selecting market segments across all media. It would also be location-sensitive and scalable from the local to the global.

While the keyword auction may yet prove to be one of the most profound innovations of search media, the problem of 'click fraud' has generated serious uncertainty for the future of pay-per-click charging (Oser 2005). Click fraud occurs when a person, or automated program, clicks on an advertiser's links to make them appear more popular than they are. It is typically initiated by a website affiliated to a search media advertising sales network to boost income. Alternatively, it is perpetrated by advertisers to exhaust rivals' budgets (Anon 2006a). Fraudulent clicks have been estimated to range from 15 to 30 per cent of all clicks (Anon 2006b; Grow *et al.* 2006), and to have cost advertisers as much as $US800 million in 2005 (Boslet 2006). A number of advertisers have initiated legal action to recover money lost to click fraud from search media (Grow *et al.* 2006). In addition to out-of-court settlements, the major search media have committed to the ongoing development of proprietary technologies to prevent click fraud, to help advertisers identify invalid clicks and to make the pay-per-click process more transparent. At the time of writing, Google was also experimenting with a new 'cost-per-action' pricing mechanism. In effect, this resembles a commission for every transaction that occurs subsequent to a prospect clicking through to an advertiser's website. Although 'cost-per-action' shows promise, it also has pitfalls, one of which is advertiser reluctance to supply search media with sensitive information about sales and leads (Boslet 2006).

The shift in search advertising pricing models from page impressions to actions shows how search media can radically narrow the gap between advertisers and customers. Broadcast television is, in comparison, quite remote from the point of transaction. Coupled with its strong connection to visual culture, television developed as a platform for innovation in creative techniques of brand promotion. There is also a view that consumers perceive global search engine brands such as Yahoo! and Google to be quite remote from a transaction. While Yahoo! and Google are quite distinctive in terms of business orientation, organizational culture and market position, they share a number of common traits, including the fact that they trade on their *global* reach. The third search media considered here illustrates a different approach to mining the *local* possibilities of advertising-funded search media, and provides an interesting point of contrast with Yahoo! and Google.

Sensis is wholly owned by Telstra, Australia's largest telecommunications carrier and, until the mid-1980s, was the monopoly provider. As part of its public service remit, Telstra maintained telephone directories and distributed them to all Australian local call areas. It also provided advertising services to businesses through its *Yellow Pages* directories. The world over, these types of directories have proven to be 'stable, recession-proof businesses that grow in line with the economy' (Sainsbury and Clow 2006). The global value of directories was estimated to be a $US25 billion in 2001 (Raphael *et al.* 2003: 1684–5). Sensis revenues were $AUD1.3 billion in 2004 (Telstra 2004: 19). This was equivalent to approximately 10 per cent of all Australian main media advertising expenditure in the same year. Advertising and directory listings were worth more to Telstra in 2004 than declining national call revenues (worth $AUD1.1 billion) and almost as much as local telephone call revenues ($AUD1.5 billion), where Telstra still retained a monopoly.

Perhaps the first true search media, telephone directories are an important advertising medium for local, small and medium-sized advertisers. Because the telephone is an essential tool of business, telephone companies have also been historically well-placed to successfully convince those that may not otherwise do so, to advertise. In the main, however, telephone companies were curiously slow to use new information and communications technologies to improve directory services. This was one consequence of a larger tension that Manuel Castells (2002: 26–7) attributes to the development of global private data networks from the 1970s. These only became viable with the development of internet-type protocols that were also being used to integrate research networks in the USA. Private networks, including private research networks, challenged the legitimacy of the market monopoly as the natural way to organize national telecommunications systems, which was particularly pronounced in the European approach to state-owned telecommunications infrastructure. The French Minitel system, established in 1982, was an important exception to the prevailing hiatus in the development of public data networks of this time. Unlike the internet, Minitel was based on principles of centralized government ownership and control.

Although the internet ultimately won out, the Minitel initiative also provided a model for addressing the various limitations of hard copy directories, including their bulk, high production and distribution costs, and problems of disposal. Database-driven, networked solutions to these problems offered a number of advantages, such as timely updating rather than updating dictated by the demands of an annual production cycle. They also paved the way for this form of public information service to be transformed into a significant new commercial media asset in a competitive telecommunications market. Because competition reduces carriage services to commodity status, information-based value added services emerge as the new sources of opportunity for developing new revenue streams. The commercial value of online directories, derived in the first instance from public switched telephone networks, arises from the array of benefits they can deliver to advertisers – especially small advertisers – as Sensis Marketing Manager, Natalie Milnes, explains:

> From an advertiser's perspective what you used to have to do, and still do, is buy an ad in the book for 12 months at a flat rate up-front without knowing if you were going to recoup the costs of that ad. For small businesses in particular, where they don't make those sorts of decisions lightly, they need to have a fair degree of confidence that they are going to get their money back, or that the benefit is going to outweigh the cost. So search marketing is fantastic in that sense because there is almost no risk. You know that everybody who clicks on your listing is a qualified lead. They are actually looking to purchase. That's why they have clicked on your listing. You don't have to worry about segmentation because they self-segment by virtue of the fact that they are after your products and services. And when they click through you are paying a

> pretty minimal fee, and that's a lead you then have ultimate control over in terms of whether you can convert that to a sale. So it's quite a different proposition to anything we have ever had before. The other thing about search is that it's probably the first relationship that's been a 'win-win-win' situation for everybody involved, from the user to the small business person who is advertising in them, to the service provider. The user gets a relevant outcome for their search. The advertiser obviously gets a qualified lead and the service provider gets the revenue that's associated with that. It's quite a balanced relationship and doesn't sacrifice the user's needs in order to just generate revenue.
>
> (Nathalie Milnes, interview 11 August 2005)

In an increasingly competitive telecommunications environment, carriers around the world spun off their directories as separate businesses in the process of updating network technologies. Telstra has followed this pattern, but now is an exception to the broader global trend for carriers to sell their directories, albeit reluctantly. In recent years many carriers, heavily burdened by debt taken on to finance investment in cell phone spectrum licences, have been compelled to sell their yellow pages companies because these, 'turned out to be their only saleable assets' (Sainsbury and Clow 2006). A private equity firm acquired Britain's *Yell* in 2001. Other private equity firms have since acquired Qwest Dex in the USA, BCE Canada's *Yellow Pages*, Singtel's Singapore directories and France's *Pages Jeune* (Sainsbury and Clow 2006).

Sensis does not aspire to the global profile of either Yahoo! or Google. Instead, its strategy is to position itself at a narrower point in the 'search funnel' than its global competitors. While consumers may use search engines for a variety of purposes, they tend to use only a very small number of search engines. Advertisers, on the other hand, use search advertising to drive traffic and transactions. Sensis wants to be the search engine Australians use when they want to make a transaction, rather than the search engine they use for other types of searches. To this end, Sensis has been acquiring media properties that help to build its location-based, e-commerce and m-commerce potential. Sensis now faces the challenge of integrating into a seamless online experience properties such as the dedicated classified publications of *The Trading Post*, which are produced in hard copy and online; the *UBD* Street Directories; as well as the *White* and *Yellow Pages*.

Another important informational form of advertising that has been rapidly migrating online is classified advertising. Online classified advertising is probably as old as internet news groups. As the internet opened up to commercial users, classified advertising began to appear on the Web in ever-expanding volumes. The relatively short-lived private networks of CompuServe, Prodigy and AOL also allowed, and in some cases encouraged, the posting of classifieds. In the mid-1990s, computer software giants such as Microsoft and internet start-ups established Web-based services that systematically targeted the three major classified advertising categories of employment, automobiles and real estate.

Online recruitment services provided by agencies such as Seek, CareerBuilder and Monster, are attractive both to job seekers and human resource managers because of the enhancements they provide, including CV and searching services. The online service is often a more convenient, faster and cheaper way for prospective employers and employees to appraise each other, particularly in younger, more socially and geographically mobile professional employment markets. Although print media still has certain advantages in the area of recruitment – mainly its capacity to capture the attention of 'passive' job seekers – the response to online employment classifieds has been impressive (Tomlinson 2002, 17–19). The number of jobs being advertised online now routinely significantly outstrips the numbers of employment classifieds appearing in newspapers (for example, Olivier Recruitment Group 2002: 7, 26).

Online classified services in the automobile category have also proven to be extraordinarily successful alternatives to printed classifieds for matching up new and second-hand car dealers, buyers and sellers, 'due in large part to dissatisfaction with dealers and the traditional car buying process' (Rayport and Jaworski 2002: 140). Similarly, online real estate classifieds not only offer enhanced and more detailed information about properties, for example, in the form of virtual tours, but they also minimize the amount of contact that buyers and renters need to have with real estate agents. The internet has made it possible to integrate access to other services, for example finance and insurance services, in ways that are relevant to classified users. There also appears to have been extraordinary growth in the personal classifieds category in the past decade or so. An increasing number of people clearly augment or substitute physical meeting places with print and online personal classifieds, in search of intimate connection (for example Moore 1998; Arvidsson 2006).

These examples illustrate the trend to disintermediation that characterizes the new services economy. Buyers and sellers find new ways to interact, often bypassing established intermediaries in various service industry value chains, including modern media, altering business models and restructuring industries in the process (Flew 2002: 64ff., 106). Google, for instance, has taken measures to change the advertising value chain in ways that reduce the opportunities for agency involvement. Google pays rebates directly to advertisers for placing their adverts with Google, instead of rewarding agencies with commissions for clients they bring to Google. This is a major break with dominant mass media remuneration practices where agencies have both sold media to advertisers and advertisers to media.

Agencies argue that Google's new agency remuneration model favours large advertising clients, and that it potentially discriminates against small advertisers because they have little choice but to deal directly with Google (Sinclair 2005). Importantly, consumers drive online advertising as much as small advertisers do, as developments in classified advertising illustrate. Indeed, the ease with which consumers can themselves advertise is a major attraction of search-based trading. People are choosing to use new media in new ways, to access more flexible services that offer an expanded range of choices for social connection, and on more convenient terms.

Getting small advertisers to actually advertise has historically been a difficult task for a variety of reasons. The comparatively large sales forces required by industrial mass media to reach small advertisers means that they are not particularly cost-effective. For this reason, small advertisers have often been neglected or taken for granted in the modern commercial media and agency industry structure. This evolved to serve a hierarchy of advertisers with global and national advertisers at the apex, sub-national and local advertisers in the middle and small businesses and individuals at the bottom. Innovations such as pay-per-click keyword advertising have provided small advertisers with new opportunities to compete on more equal terms with larger advertisers for national, indeed global, reach.

Search media are having a significant impact on the shape and content of the mass-circulation newspaper. Search media such as Yahoo!, Google and Sensis have achieved significant efficiencies in managing small, classified advertisers. Along with numerous online classified specialists, they now compete with newspapers, especially metropolitan daily newspapers, where classifieds can account for anywhere between 30 and 60 per cent of revenue. Although the consequences of these shifts in classified advertising for the print media are ominous, they are also highly variable (Spurgeon 2003). While certain types of newspaper may disappear from our communication ecologies, others may yet flourish and prosper. Metropolitan daily newspapers have been hit particularly hard by classified advertising losses to online media, but national newspapers are less likely to be as adversely affected. Free, highly localized, community-based newspapers are proliferating in many conurbations. These developments also reflect the impact of globalization on media consumption preferences, which favour more 'glocal' patterns of identification (Robertson 1994). Other, newer, online publishers also share in the twin benefits that search media have facilitated: becoming more discoverable and having access to growing online advertising revenue streams. It is useful to return to the Google example to illustrate how this occurs.

Google offers two main advertising services. AdWords is a keyword auctioning service that provides a range of advertising management tools, including performance monitoring and reporting. It is designed to be a self-service program. One small new media enterprise that reported great success with Google AdWords was

Radio LabourStart. Launched by the Web-based labour activist group of the same name in 2004, and streamed from AOL's Live365 server, Radio LabourStart promoted itself through an email drop to LabourStart's 18,000 subscribers around the world. The initial response was strong, but the numbers soon began to drop off. In an effort to lift its listenership, Radio LabourStart used Google keywords to advertise in association with the names of many of the performers featured in playlists. LabourStart's founding editor and self-published author, Eric Lee, describes the results of the campaign in the following terms:

> In the first seven months of the Google ads being shown, the ads were displayed a staggering 2.3 million times, at a cost of only $700. Over 14,300 visitors were attracted to the radio station (that's around 2000 per month) while searching for Bob Dylan or Phil Ochs or Joan Baez.
>
> (Lee 2005: 44–5)

In addition to appearing in Google search results, advertiser access to the inventory of online media can also be managed through AdWords. Online publishers, large and small, use this service if they want their inventory brokered by Google. It is organized as an affiliate program and uses contextual search algorithms to match advertising to keywords appearing in other online media. It also dynamically distributes this advertising content to affiliated websites and publishers, many of whom would not otherwise have the capacity to sell or manage advertising. Affiliates earn income for this advertising and can exercise control over the process. For example, they can specify minimum rates and intervene at various points to address the sometimes surprising consequences of contextual advertising (for example, to relocate the Samsonite luggage ad that was served adjacent to a story about body parts being found in a suitcase). While contextual search was another of Google's important contributions to search-based advertising, the affiliated sales network has proven problematic, allowing click-fraud perpetrators to find their way into the Google network.

Services such as Google AdWords and AdSense nevertheless provide a means by which businesses of all sizes can generate new revenue streams, but proliferating micro and small businesses are potentially their greatest beneficiaries. They can acquire professional media services with relative ease, which, in turn, frees resources that can be dedicated to the core business. Larger online publishers have also reported that contextual advertising enables them to generate revenues for types of news, entertainment and sports pages that they have found difficult to sell directly to advertisers.

Search media thus seem to emerge as the heroes of diversity in the brave new online media world. Their Long Tail dynamics make them natural allies with small advertisers and informational advertising techniques. But to what extent can search media really be expected to remain focused on the visibility and viability of small media and small business? Small advertisers are certainly more numerous, and search media make it cost-effective to scale access for year-round, self-managed small advertiser activity. Small advertisers can theoretically take advantage of the keyword auction system to buy hundreds of thousands of obscure search terms, as well as space on numerous highly targeted affiliate websites, for negligible costs. It seems, however, that this is one point where the end of the Long Tail comes into sight. Google now limits the number of active keywords that an AdWords account may have at any given time to 50,000. This has given rise to speculation that Google would in fact prefer to provide services for a large number of advertisers competing for small numbers of niche keywords and search terms (Veiner 2005). The potential for major search media and national advertisers to influence the dimensions of the Long Tail is significant. In 2004 the top ten search media companies accounted for 74 per cent of online advertising expenditures in the USA (PWC 2005: 7). In the same year, national advertisers were reported to be the largest online advertisers, accounting for 94 per cent of online advertising expenditure, compared to only 6 per cent for local advertisers (PWC 2005: 11). While the rhetoric of new media suggests that all citizen consumers are now also advertisers, the emerging reality looks somewhat different. The strategic value of small advertisers to the new search media is certainly considerable. However, the economic value of small, local advertisers does not begin to approach that of large national advertisers. The economic case for global search media to organize around the requirements of large advertisers may ultimately prove as irresistible as it was for modern mass media.

'Madison and Vine': trends in brand advertising

Digitization potentially makes all media highly searchable. This is because digitization allows the locus of control in media distribution systems to reside with end-users, not just at system hubs. Search interfaces facilitate greater end-user control over media and entertainment choices, and are daily increasing in sophistication. For example, electronic programme guides that support so-called personal video recorders (PVRs) are rapidly developing, often in association with the digitization of media communications infrastructure. A number of these applications enable consumers to remove advertisements in their entirety in the process of discovering and time-shifting television programmes. These developments present major challenges for advertisers. They are similarly problematic for media, which need to convince advertisers that they can deliver the desired audiences. They also come quickly on the heels of other important changes set in train from the 1980s, which saw mass media audiences begin to fragment. Accompanying the growth of multi-channel subscription television, especially in North America and Europe, national advertiser interest grew in the capacity of new niche media to support targeted signalling and customization over the ability of modern media to bring people together (Turow 2000). Advertiser interest in mass media began to wane, and budgets began to be rebalanced in line with a renewed interest in a range of marketing communication methods other than advertising.

National advertisers and global brands began to move away from upfront spending in advertising through mass media to invest in niche media and branded content. As already discussed in the introduction to this chapter, branded content covers a wide spectrum of activities, including product placements, infomercials, sponsorships and content creation. It also has a long and diverse history (Galician 2004). Armand Mattelart traces a continuum in the development of branded content from the time that the first American advertising agency, N.W. Ayer & Son, restructured in 1928 to take advantage of the possibilities of radio advertising. J. Walter Thompson was also a prolific early producer of advertiser-funded radio network programming in the USA, and when the world's largest advertiser, Proctor & Gamble, took direct control of radio production, a new radio genre – the 'soap opera' – was created (Mattelart 2002: 125–7). Advertising time bartering practices that emerged in the late 1980s stimulated advertiser and agency interest in television programme production. There are many variations of barter, but the basic principle is simple, as Mattelart explains:

> a transmission is provided ready-made to a television channel by an advertiser or advertising agency in exchange for advertising screening time instead of money. The agency uses this space for its clients . . ..
>
> (2002: 127)

Television schedules are filled with numerous examples of advertiser-funded and produced entertainment. Production of the Australian version of the Endemol-owned format programme *Ready Steady Cook* is substantially funded by the independent I&G supermarket chain. Sensis produces a small business magazine programme *Bread*, which is also broadcast on Australian network television. Other recent examples include *The Restaurant*, a format which is part funded by American Express; *The Grill*, a ten-part series broadcast on UK Channel 4 and funded by PlayStation 2; and *Blow Out*, a fully funded barter arrangement on the US cable network Bravo (Gallagher 2004).

Of interest here is the recent intensification of national advertiser interest in the production of branded entertainment. This can be understood as an important creative response to the growth of search culture. It is based on the development of strategic alliances between advertisers and entertainment companies and often bypasses main media altogether. Branded entertainment aims to contextualize brand images in ways that are so appealing that consumers will seek them out for inclusion in their personalized media and entertainment flows. More recently, branded entertainment initiatives have shifted in focus from niche marketing to brand community-building. The role that advertiser-fear of the impact of search interfaces such as PVRs has played in the current rush to invest in branded entertainment has been well-documented by Scott Donaton, who coined the term 'Madison and Vine' to describe this trend (Donaton 2004).

BMW made one of the most dramatic recent forays into branded entertainment. Acting on the advice of its advertising agency, and drawing on its earlier experience with product placement in James Bond movies, BMW Films was established to make and distribute a series of ads for BMW that took the form of short films. Internationally acclaimed creative teams were put together with some of Hollywood's best producers, directors and actors. Creative control was passed over to the production team and the internet was used as the main medium of distribution. Electronic word-of-mouth was the principal means for publicizing the films.[1] With an estimated budget of $US15 million, BMW Films successfully brought BMW into direct contact with a highly desirable demographic of affluent, young, new media users, not easily reached by conventional advertising means. BMW Films produced an immediate spike in sales followed by year-on-year increases for 2001–03, despite a sharp downturn in the US economy in this period. According to Donaton, a number of advertising's sacred cows became BMW Films' road-kill. For example, instead of spending 10 per cent on production and 90 per cent on distribution, BMW films reversed these budget ratios.

Where BMW Films modelled convergence for the advertising and the film industry, an earlier partnership between Sting and Jaguar modelled convergence for the advertising and the music industries, even though this partnership came about by accident rather than design. The video clip, produced in 2000 for the title single from Sting's album, *Desert Rose*, featured the pop star being chauffeured through the desert in an S-Type Jaguar. On previewing the clip, Sting's manager realized that they had unintentionally produced an ad for Jaguar. The promotional budget for Sting's album was effectively increased from $US1.8 million to $US18.9 million when Jaguar agreed, through its New York advertising agency Ogilvy & Mather, to use the video clip as the basis of a global campaign that included a major TV advertising commitment. The reported results of this partnership were extraordinary (Donaton 2004: 142). Where previously the single had struggled for airplay, radio stations were inundated with requests, and the album went on to sell 8 million copies worldwide. Jaguar sales increased fourfold and the median age of buyers dropped.

The trend to branded entertainment has been controversial for a number of reasons. Within advertising, BMW Films has added fuel to a heated debate about whether branded entertainment should be regarded as advertising. This tension is illustrated by the fact that BMW Films' entry in the film section of the Cannes international advertising festival was refused, while the series has since been included in the permanent collection of New York's Museum of Modern Art (Donaton 2004: 103–4). Branded entertainment perpetuates the blurring of the distinction between commerce and art, and popular culture and public culture. Branded entertainment also contributes to the movement of advertisers and associated revenues away from main media. Although the overall amount that national advertisers spend on marketing and advertising continues to grow, a rebalancing within these budgets is also occurring. Increasing proportions of national advertising budgets are being diverted to branded entertainment. Sometimes these budgets are reinvested in network and multichannel television content, in new forms that aim to break through the surrounding clutter and to engage consumers in refreshing ways. Sometimes they are diverted away from television altogether. It is also apparent that branded entertainment alliances between advertisers and entertainment companies are shifting in focus from niche marketing to online initiatives in building branded communities.

In the past few years, Coca-Cola's marketing strategy has made increasing use of branded entertainment as a way of dealing with the twin challenges of media fragmentation and proliferation, and escalating media and sponsorship costs. The enduring success of this brand in maintaining its place at the top of the international brand league table in the face of considerable gains by new media challenger Microsoft, has been attributed to localized approaches to delivering Coca-Cola's centrally devised brand message (Berner and Kiley 2005: 86–94). The Coca-Cola website, from which it is possible to visit the websites of any of the 100 or more territories in which the company operates, provides a good illustration of the strategy.[2] While basic brand elements such as logo and colour are always consistent, there can be considerable variation in website content from country to country. Ceding control over marketing to branch offices has enabled a localized approach to developing and maintaining brand communities. It also constitutes a globally distributed marketing innovation system for Coca-Cola. Local successes in the area of branded entertainment and community-building are being adapted to facilitate the move beyond advertiser-funded television programming in other local markets.

Since Atlanta's move to a 'glocal' corporate communication and branding structure (Roberts 2001), Coca-Cola in Australia has been developing a branded entertainment and community-building strategy that leverages teenagers' interest in live music. It has expanded quickly from a number of modest alcohol-free, live music events for under 18-year-olds to a major effort to cohere a community of brand users through a shared love of music. It integrates a programme of live concerts with promotional activity at numerous targeted touchpoints, including sponsorship of video hits programmes on multichannel TV, cinema advertising, FM radio spots, the Coca-Cola website, SMS marketing, packaging and point of sale. Coca-Cola in Australia has used new media elements to explore the potential for personalizing the brand relationship with consumers. In 2000 it ran Australia's first SMS promotion, which reportedly attracted over 2 million entries (Sophocleous 2003). In other years the ticketing process required concert-goers to register online with Coca-Cola. Up to 49,000 people attended these events in 2003 and 2004 (Eaton 2004). While the results of this particular integrated branded entertainment strategy have not been fully disclosed, this sort of direct contact provides advertisers with the opportunity to build very valuable databases and market profiles that can be used on a continuing basis. Atlanta was reportedly so impressed with the Australian innovation that decisions were taken to roll out the strategy in the UK, Germany and France (Messer 2004).

Another example of a branded entertainment alliance that is intently focused on building and sustaining a brand community is provided by the co-branding of a high-end line of Nike runners with the Apple iPod. Apple developed a radio-frequency identification (RFID) device that enables the iPod Nano to interconnect with footwear and which supports applications designed to enhance the running experience. Nike was the first brand to incorporate the technology into Nike-branded runners. An RFID sensor, placed inside a Nike+ shoe, interfaces wirelessly with the Nano to generate real time data on the exercise effort, including run duration, distance and energy consumption. The product is supported by a website where Nike+ users can build their own training profile, set and monitor personal goals and compare progress with other Nike+ users. Forums allow community members to ask and answer questions about the product, as well as share a passion for running. The website allows communities of runners to discuss personal and collective challenges, create a running leaderboard and cooperate in various ways, for example in the organization of runs. They can also share playlist information, and buy Apple iTunes and other Nike and Apple branded products and accessories. The site also interfaces with Google Maps so that community members can share route details.

What distinguishes the Nike+ initiative from the other examples of branded entertainment considered so far is that in this instance end-users provide the bulk of the site's content. Nike aggregates the necessary community infrastructure in the form of communications tools and the Web interface. Community members do the rest, and are converted into brand owners and advocates in the process. But even here unruly consumers do not always behave as the brands intend them to. For example, one inventive iPod fan quickly discovered that they could attach the sensor to a different and, in their opinion, more comfortable pair of running shoes, and publicized this modification on their iPod fan blog.[3]

Numerous new online media enterprises that mix the intercreative features of multi-user online games and virtual communities are proliferating as brand intermediaries, from Second Life to NeoPets. Habbo Hotel is one such destination designed to appeal to teenagers.[4] It resembles a cross between The Sims and a chat room. Its publisher, Finnish company Sulake, promotes Habbo Hotel as a safe virtual meeting place and site for positive self-expression. Since going live in 2000, Habbo Hotel visitors have created over 30 million avatars, known as 'Habbos'. Habbo Hotel does not rely on standard advertising methods to grow its user base. Instead, it has adapted the referral model to its new media environment. It promotes a recruitment incentive scheme to existing members, and relies on the viral spread of news about Habbo to drive new memberships. Existing Habbo members are rewarded with Habbo credits for each new Habbo member they recruit. Sulake claims a monthly total of 3.7 million unique visitors to the 16 Habbo Hotels located on different national internet domains. Fan communities have established themselves around Habbo Hotels. A number of these are Habbo-endorsed, including one that streams fan-produced radio shows. These fan sites are regularly monitored for insights into a range of issues, including how Habbo Hotels might grow advertising revenue streams in its existing in-game, user-pays economy. While it is not necessary to make any purchases to create a Habbo avatar or to participate in the basic Habbo Hotel service, Habbo Hotels presently generate most of their income from in-game sales of virtual furniture that Habbos can purchase to decorate their rooms. It aims to build advergaming as a way of diversifying revenue. This includes corporate sponsorship of virtual spaces and events within the local Habbo Hotel. It also extends to the creation of in-game bots that are programmed to offer positive messages about a sponsor's products and services. The Habbo network also supports international promotions. For example, in September 2005 the virtual hip-hop band Gorillaz undertook a virtual promotional world tour of 12 Habbo Hotels. Fans could attend the virtual concerts and there were competitions for a variety of sponsored prizes, including virtual backstage passes and tickets to Gorillaz press conferences.

Defining new commercial media

This discussion of the influence of search culture on developments in informational and creative approaches to advertising has tended to use advertising revenues to delimit new commercial media from other Web-based activities such as e-commerce. For example, the global auction house eBay has not been discussed, even though a form of enhanced, search-based classified advertising lies at the heart of its business. This is because eBay principally generates its earnings from the percentage share on sales, which also has major consequences for the juridical context and orientation of the business. While the operational distinction made here between commercial online media and e-commerce services helps to make the scope of this investigation manageable, it is also highly porous.

Consider also the example of Amazon.com, which is rapidly developing into a universal electronic catalogue. Providing third party seller access to its catalogue pages is an increasingly important part of Amazon's business. It is conceivable that Amazon could evolve into the world's largest Web-based shopping channel and be regarded, primarily, as a form of commercial media. For the moment, however, Amazon's revenues overwhelmingly come from the sales of products and services to its global website customers, so it is not framed here as new commercial media. Conversely, Yahoo! is principally an advertising-funded search medium for now, but may not always be so if it succeeds in repositioning itself as a premium rate broadband entertainment portal. The corporate websites considered here still largely have the soft sell feel of self-interested public relations and marketing, but some could conceivably emerge as significant branded media content channels.

Similarly, the creative advertisement is not a stable category. Trends in branded content have seen it break free of the confines of the 30-second broadcast spot or the print media display ad. It includes product placement, programme production, advergaming, brand communities, entertainment, cool hunting and more. Adam Arvidsson argues that many of these techniques aim to commodify 'the autonomous productivity of consumers as it unfolds naturally' in the social environment (Arvidsson 2006: 15). They aim to enlist the affective labour of consumers in adding intrinsic value to the qualities of a brand, in the spontaneous processes of everyday communication (Arvidsson 2006: 69). The range of activities that comprise branded content, and those of the even larger sweep of brand management, do not seem problematic for advertising critics who have tended to include all aspects of promotional culture within the ambit of advertising (Wernick 1991; Mosco 1996: 107–8). However, this generalization can be a major issue for the advertising industry and its highly specialized areas of knowledge and professional practice ('disciplines' to industry insiders). New commercial media contribute to the disruption of these disciplines as well as the underlying business of advertising. Selling mass media to advertisers was the industry's core business for most of the twentieth century, with commissions from these sales providing the main source of agency income. While mass media commissions are still the mainstay of advertising income, many agencies now generate income from a raft of other services, including fees for creative services. The addition of new media to the media mix is an important factor that shifts the balance of power away from the agencies to advertisers and consumers in the global era.

Search media offer small advertisers affordable market reach and potentially shorten the length of the transaction funnel – the point between learning about a particular good or service and actually buying it. The impact of advertising in these environments is measurable and often demonstrable and, importantly, is supported by data on performance. Search media optimize informational advertising by enhancing its discoverability and relevance. Because end-users actively seek out the information (rather than selecting from whatever is served up) these media are able to capitalize on the value of non-editorial content to end-users. As Peter Morris astutely observes, they break 'the nexus between news and advertising, thus fracturing the synergies created by the invention of the newspaper' (Morris 1996: 16). Credibility, as an information source, can be just as important to search media as it is to agenda-setting news media. So too are the qualities of accuracy, integrity, reliability and timeliness.

Branded content initially harnessed creative resources of communication professionals to remediate the problems of advertising clutter and commercial interruption associated with mass media. It explored new consumer touchpoints and new promotional alliances. This included branded entertainment for targeted segments of niche media consumers. Tentative experiments with the intercreative capacity of networked end-users to create branded content are also now apparent. Examples such as Nike+ suggest that the creative credibility of branded content is a matter that might exercise the minds of advertisers in much the same way that informational credibility concerns search media.

In evaluating these trends, care has been taken to avoid the well-worn groove produced by earlier debates about the social merits of advertising. These earlier debates have provided important commentaries on the co-adaptation of advertising and mass media but they have generated judgements about informational and creative approaches to advertising that are not particularly helpful to understanding the role of advertising in the commercialization of new media. The aim here, instead, has been to consider the ways in which new media and advertising continue to co-adapt.

Chapter 3

Integrating interactivity

Globalization and the gendering of creative advertising

In October 2005, Neil French, the consulting creative director for one of the world's largest advertising and marketing services conglomerates, WPP, was forced to resign in the backlash to sexist comments he made at a Toronto industry event. In responding to a question about why there are so few women creative directors in advertising, French used very colourful language to argue that men are better at the creative dimensions of advertising than are women. Men, he said, are more willing and able to live for work, while women are more inclined to work to live. According to French, the demands of pregnancy and child-rearing compromise the creative capacity of women to the extent that they are not generally well-suited to creative work in advertising. For most industry insiders there was nothing out of the ordinary about this point of view; it was consistent with a particular gendering of creativity that has become the norm in creative agency work culture. For this reason, the global debate that French's comments sparked took many industry folk by surprise, including the highly regarded creative luminary himself.[1] French had not anticipated the extent to which the industry was ripe for an opportunity to debate women's participation in advertising as creatives, or the strength of opinion, expressed in the online conversations initiated by a new breed of blog-enabled citizen-journalists (Bruns and Jacobs 2006), which precipitated French's resignation.

Conversational media mean consumers are more able to engage directly with each other and advertisers and, consequently, are not as reliant on advertising texts for information. Furthermore, consumers generally perceive consumer-generated word-of-mouth, now electronically dispersed along viral paths, to be a more reliable source of information than marketing communication, including advertising (Blackshaw and Nazzaro 2004). The capacity to establish, maintain and extend dialogic relations with consumers – within and beyond marketing communication forms – now carries a premium. Yet, as far as creative practice is concerned, it seems that advertising is not as well equipped to converse with female target groups as it is with male counterparts. The challenge of re-imagining the feminized consumer as an active constituent of markets and marketing communication remains apparent in advertising codes of representation and in industry practices of participation. Sex and gender stereotyping, as well as women's participation in the industry, are longstanding sites of controversy in advertising, and are the focus of important feminist critiques of advertising texts and industry practices.

In this chapter, a comparative case study of two global advertising campaigns extends these debates into the broader consideration of the implications of conversational media for advertising. This analysis draws attention to the influence of globalization on advertising industry culture and creative advertising strategies in particular, as well as the disruptive potential of conversational media for the prevailing gender relations of advertising. The particular norms of gendered creativity reflected in French's comments are located in advertising's 'third wave' of internationalization (Mattelart 2002: 3) and creativity (Cronin 2000; Mort 1996). The institutional and textual implications of this view of creativity for advertising are demonstrable. So too is the wider significance of French's declaration that his resignation amounted to 'death by blog' (Canning 2005) for the co-adaptation of advertising and new media.

Importantly, the influence of globalization means that prevailing norms of gendered creativity are not limited to advertising. The assumption that creativity is an attribute of youthful masculinity is endemic in many industries that rely heavily on creative labour inputs (Nixon 2003).

The creative achievements of advertising targeted to men have dominated international industry awards for decades (Berman *et al.* 2006). The absence of breakthrough creative work targeted at women is an issue that has been raised by women within the industry on various occasions.[2] The 2004 findings of a major multi-country study undertaken by Leo Burnett Worldwide confirmed that women widely perceive ads intended for them to be less interesting than those for men in equivalent categories (LBW 2004; Berman *et al.* 2006). Although they are thought to be responsible for up to 80 per cent of all buying decisions across most consumer categories, the study concluded that women, or more precisely the advertising clients who want to reach them, are underserved by creative advertising. At best, the creative work of advertising fails to motivate or move women to the extent that it does men and, at worst, it remains cliché-ridden, uninspiring or offensive.

The Leo Burnett study showed that advertising in many key categories such as financial services and automotive trade still fails to acknowledge that the economic status of women has changed and that women are increasingly in control of household spending, if not financially independent. The study challenged the outdated perceptions of women consumers that continue to inform a lot of advertising, and aimed to educate the industry in the finer details of the use of a variety of creative appeals in advertising to women. It found that although women were quite adept at ignoring sexist advertising, sex can be used to sell to women as effectively as men if it is 'approached with a distinctly female point of view' (LBW 2004). It also found that women respond well to emotions, but only when they are truly moving. Similarly, characters and situations represented in ads need to be plausible if they are to attract and hold women's interest. But the big news flash of the study was that women liked to laugh and wanted to see greater use of humour in commercials created for them.

The Leo Burnett study was a highly diplomatic rendering of a difficult issue for many industry women. It offered a valuable industry perspective on present limits of creative advertising, not just in what it said, but also in its silences. It stopped short of asking why advertising creative departments are apparently so resistant to engaging with the changing socio-economic status of women, and it avoided any exploration of the relationship between the persistence of these blind spots, misconceptions and outdated perceptions and possible structural or cultural explanations for why creative appeals frequently do not work for women.

A range of explanatory factors has been identified in cultural studies of advertising over the past couple of decades. These include the problems of structural discrimination that persist in agency employment practices and the 'Peter Pan' culture that pervades many creative departments. The privileging of masculine myths of creativity has been enormously productive in unlocking new male consumer markets over the past quarter century. Creative innovation in textual address has been found to be strongly associated with male-targeted advertisements (Cronin 2000). At the level of workplace relations, however, industry-wide, structural inequities, produced and re-produced in the work practices and cultures of creative advertising agencies, have also had significant exclusionary consequences for women. There is a certain irony here. As the following case study of the Axe/Lynx brand of male toiletries shows, the strength of creative advertising in its third wave iteration is derived from practices of knowing consumers and consumption that are meaning-oriented and based on cultural dialogue. In this way, creative advertising has provided powerful solutions to advertisers faced by the imperative of fragmenting media to diversify the types, not just the points, of intercreative connection that can be made with consumers. Yet, between French's comments and the Leo Burnett study, it seems that the scope and capacity of creative advertising to support the modes of communication and cultural exchange that have been immensely successful for a male-targeted brand such as Axe/Lynx does not often extend beyond the cultural milieux that advertising creatives themselves also occupy (Soar 2000). The case of another global Unilever brand, Dove, provides an interesting point of contrast to the Axe/Lynx strategy and serves to illustrate some of the additional challenges that creative advertising faces in overcoming the limits of gendered notions of creativity.

Dove and the Axe/Lynx effect

With an estimated global advertising expenditure of $US3.5 billion in 2004, Unilever ranks as the third largest advertiser in the world after Proctor & Gamble and General Motors.[3] The Anglo–Dutch conglomerate has been credited with being the first packaged goods manufacturer in the world, and is still one of the largest. Since the late 1990s, Unilever has been consolidating its diverse portfolio. This has involved a number of major takeovers and the simultaneous rationalization of its brand portfolios to concentrate on a smaller number of global 'power' brands. These are managed in two divisions: Unilever Bestfoods, which is the home of Unilever's food and beverages brands, and Unilever Home & Personal care, which houses global brands including Dove and Axe (marketed as Lynx in the UK and Australia and henceforth referred to as 'Axe/Lynx'). Other brands owned by Unilever include Flora, Lipton and various ice cream and frozen food brands in food and beverages, and Omo, Persil and Rexona/Sure in home and personal care. The similarities, as well as the differences, between the creative branding strategies for Axe/Lynx and Dove make them intrinsically interesting case studies for a comparative analysis of contemporary developments in the uses of sex, gender and stereotyping in advertising, as well as the gendering of creativity in advertising creative practice. Both have successfully drawn from the cultural resources of the target markets themselves to redefine popular notions of masculine sex appeal (in the case of Axe/Lynx) and feminine beauty (in the case of Dove). They also rely heavily on various creative, iterative, conversational strategies and tactics to constantly refresh their image. Yet both brands make quite contrary contributions to broader questions about the role of advertising in the social shaping of women's status. Dove deals directly with the critiques of female representation that have dogged advertising for more than a quarter of a century, while Axe/Lynx perpetuates them. Axe/Lynx also provides a window onto the impact of underlying structural inequalities in the employment practices of the industry. The fact that the two brands are owned and controlled by the one company highlights the extent to which sex, first and foremost, remains the richest and most versatile cultural resource available to advertising (Jhally 1990: 135).

Both brands have been associated with Unilever for a number of decades. Dove beauty soap was first developed and marketed by Unilever in the USA in 1957. Ogilvy & Mather (O&M) developed the first campaigns, which ran for over 30 years and helped make Dove the top-selling cleansing soap in the world. O&M still hold the Dove account worldwide. From the mid-1980s, Unilever began to develop Dove brand extensions such as deodorants, body washes and hair products. At about this time, Unilever also set about creating a toiletries brand that would appeal to a male youth market, and Axe/Lynx was born. Although it became the leading brand in its category, by the mid-1990s market research was showing that Axe/Lynx brand was dating. It was in danger of becoming 'the Brut of the 90s'. In 1995 the account was moved to Bartle Bogle Hegarty (BBH), an agency headquartered in London that, in the previous decade, had established a global reputation for its creative approach to developing male consumer markets (Mort 1996). Axe/Lynx is now sold in more than 60 countries and claims a 37 per cent share of the male deodorant category and 80 per cent of the core target market of 15- to 19-year-old males.[4]

The success of Axe/Lynx arises from the extent to which brand managers have effectively enlisted the support of the target market in the co-creation of the revitalized brand values (Arvidsson 2006), by filtering the brand proposition through their social networks and social relations. This level of consumer productivity was inspired by a laddish, tongue-in-cheek masculinity that BBH creatives struck upon in order to reconnect the brand with the sexual mores of a globalized youth culture. The key proposition of the branding strategy was that young men around the world share a common interest in the 'mating game'. The campaign creators maintained that the field of play for the game arises wherever boys and girls meet, and is made more complex as traditional notions of masculinity have come under challenge in the processes of rapid social change, including changes associated with the impact of feminism. However, anyone can play and, by preparing for play with the right kind of accessory, anyone can win. This is where Axe/Lynx-branded products, and their apparently irresistible effects on the opposite sex, can deliver the resourceful young man a decisive advantage.

The genius of the BBH strategy lay in its capacity of the underlying creative concept to engage the target market in an open-ended number of narrative possibilities for rolling campaigns, and an annual launch cycle of new after-shave scents and brand extensions that would ensure the currency of the branded products. The global concept was executed on a regional basis. Creative teams were assembled in London, New York and Singapore, three regional centres of creative excellence. Executions frequently tested, but rarely exceeded the limits of acceptable mass media representations of sex in local markets. Axe/Lynx ads have generally stayed under the radar of censors and regulators due to the calculated use of highly targeted niche media and tactical media events. This strategy contained any risk of regulatory intervention arising from unnecessary exposure of the brand to those most likely to be offended by its values.

The BBH strategy for Axe/Lynx also deliberately set about breaking with the paradigm of interruption that prevailed in mass media. It aimed instead for integration into the 'existing networks of interaction and communication' of target market subcultures (Arvidsson 2006: 69). This is illustrated by the key promotional strategy used in the UK, and implemented by leading PR agency Freud Communications, retained to build the brand's association with UK club and dance culture. In the early 2000s, the brand sponsored major dance party events in the south of Spain as well as in the UK and Ireland. These events featured top DJs and performers and were named after new Lynx fragrances, for example 'Voodoo Nights' and 'Phoenix Legends'. At the centre of the multi-award winning campaign to support the launch of the 2003 fragrance 'Pulse', was 'Make Luv', a single produced by a popular Belgian DJ and released on CD and music video. A leading popular choreographer created a dance which was also digitally rendered as screen-saver for viral internet distribution. The dance and the single provided the main elements of the television commercial (TVC), which featured an ordinary guy who relied on his dancing ability and the alluring power of Axe/Lynx to reel in two women. Both the dance and the CD became popular in clubs across the UK. The CD captured the 'number 1' spot in the UK music charts for three weeks. The 'Lynx Effect' turned into a popular cultural phenomenon as a generation of young men learned how to dance.

Key factors in the success of the BBH strategy for Axe/Lynx included the quality of the business partnership between the advertiser and agency. BBH claimed that Unilever permitted a degree of freedom with Axe/Lynx that other Unilever brands did not enjoy. The perceived differences between the young male market for Axe/Lynx and the predominantly female consumers of most Unilever brands justified a different philosophy. The suggestion of gender-based differential treatment of brands echoes the experiences of second wave feminists in establishing autonomous but, nevertheless, mainstream, advertising-funded magazines. Founding editor of *Ms Magazine* Gloria Steinem (1994) attributed many of the problems of *Ms*, and the failure of *Sassy*, its stable mate intended for younger women, to the control that advertisers sought to exercise over the editorial as well as the advertising content of women's magazines. Steinem claimed that magazines intended for male readerships did not experience the same level of interference for a complex variety of reasons. These included dominant and enduring normative expectations that commercial media targeted at women would not disrupt established gendered social orders. Advertisers consequently felt authorized to make demands of women's magazines that would not have been tolerated by men's magazines.

There also appears to have been a close alignment between the cultural capital of the creative teams involved in devising and executing the Axe/Lynx brand strategy and the aspirations of the target market. In other words, the interests and identities of these two groups were so co-extensive that their roles were potentially interchangeable. For example, one rumour aired online was that the actor in the 'Make Luv' music video and TVC was a Freud Communications principle.[5] While this was not in fact the case, it nevertheless seemed plausible that the brand agents would themselves make use of the 'The Axe/Lynx Effect' in the mating game, just as the target market had assumed responsibility for promoting it in the process of incorporating the brand into dance and club culture. The Axe/Lynx strategy exhibits the reflexivity, innovation and rapid turnover in campaigns that Anne Cronin has described as typical of male-targeted advertisements. In contrast,

> female-targeted advertisements predominantly use a 'literal' or non-reflexive form of address and have a far slower cycle of innovation. This male gendering of innovation in advertising targeting is perhaps ironic as consumer culture has consistently been figured as a feminine domain and consumer culture itself is often presented as the epitome of cultural change.
>
> (Cronin 2000: 8)

An exceptional instance of innovation in targeting female markets, the Dove 'Campaign for Real Beauty', bears out these observations.

While young men pursue women in the mating game, many brands aim to draw women into the beauty game. Changing the rules of the beauty game was the mission that O&M embarked upon in 2002 when work began on updating Dove's brand image from classic iconic to one that was 'culturally and socially relevant' to contemporary women (Gelston 2005). The new campaign kicked off in September 2004 with the launch of a multi-country study of women's attitudes to beauty, commissioned by Dove and undertaken by an international research team.[6] Findings provided the empirical basis for anchoring the brand to the proposition that beauty was within the reach of every woman, irrespective of age, size or colour. Susie Orbach, from the London School of Economics and author of *Fat is a Feminist Issue*, was one of a number of prominent feminists to advise on the supporting research and lend credibility to the central claim of the repositioning strategy: that the brand could provide a platform for engaging with real women and their concerns about the representation of beauty in advertising and the popular media.

Twelve national O&M offices were invited to experiment with local interpretations of the 'Campaign for Real Beauty' and associated campaigns for various Dove brand extensions. As also occurred with the Axe/Lynx campaigns, many of these innovations were then internationalized. For example, a Canadian exhibition of women's portraits by top female photographers toured internationally. The idea of recruiting real women of diverse shapes, sizes and colour for the 'Tested on Real Curves' campaign for Dove's skin-firming lotion in the UK, was also internationalized. A website was created to house campaign resources and to support a dialogue about the meaning of beauty. New advertising technologies that incorporated registrational interactivity were used on the website and on electronic billboards in high-traffic locations such as Times Square in New York. They featured real women as ambassadors of unconventional beauty, and invited viewers to vote via the Web or by SMS on whether they were 'Wizened or Wonderful?', 'Gray or Gorgeous?', 'Flawed or Flawless?' and so on. There were also a number of philanthropic tie-ins with eating disorder charities and educational programmes intended to build the self-esteem of school-aged girls. A formal public relations effort, which included public forums on the question of beauty, was also integral to the campaign. The high impact of the repositioning strategy was apparent in the significant amount of buzz it generated in various media and in the informal conversational networks of the internet. This included the comments of sceptics ('too bad they're hawking cellulite cream') and critics (with comments ranging from, 'I hate the idea that people are now trying to create this idea that fat is beautiful' to, 'Last I heard, making 50-foot posters of girls in their underwear isn't exactly groundbreaking'). In the main, though, the blogosphere seemed to have responded very positively to the Dove re-positioning strategy ('overall I'd give Dove and Ogilvy a massive gold star for these campaigns').[7]

Dove claims that it has always used real women in its ads rather than models. In this and other respects, the Campaign for Real Beauty did not actually represent a break with core brand values. It aimed instead to update the brand's connection to realistic rather than idealistic notions of beauty. Through realism, the brand strategy aimed to individualize, indeed democratize, popular perceptions of beauty. Because the strategy presumed a dialogic rather than a transmission communication model, some interesting control dilemmas arose. For example, *Business Week* reported that the electronic billboard in Toronto, which invited passers-by to vote on whether the woman it featured was 'Fat or Fab', was taken down when the vote for 'fat' took the lead (Gogoi 2005). Even though many of the people commenting on blogs appeared to be young women, the products themselves were perceived to be traditional and, ultimately, only of interest for women over 30. The first iteration in the Campaign for Real Beauty was very broadly targeted compared to the campaigns for Axe/Lynx. It also showed extraordinary restraint. This was also reflected in the research findings underpinning the campaign. Although significant, they were quite predictable: 'authentic beauty is a concept lodged in women's hearts and minds and seldom articulated in popular culture or affirmed in the mass media', and furthermore, 'women around the world would like to see media change in the way that it represents beauty'.[8] O&M did not have the same degree of creative freedom with Dove and its female markets that BBH had with the male markets for Axe/Lynx. It seems that while the brand managers and O&M were confident that the Real Beauty position would resonate with women they met with strong resistance from within Unilever. A promotional video was made to help sell the campaign to Unilever executives. The video 'featured the daughters of top executives revealing what characteristics they would change about themselves . . . to show how the beauty industry begins chipping away at girls' self-esteem' (Gelston 2005). It seems the public relations effort was as much about keeping Unilever executives sold on the repositioning strategy, by demonstrating popular support for it, as it was about maintaining consumer interest in the brand.

Despite these constraints, the campaign broke new ground in the use of conversational media to initiate a dialogue with women about things that matter to them. It used this dialogue to expand the cultural resource base available to women and advertisers. It also had a major bottom-line impact. With sales in excess of €2.5 billion in 80 countries, the Campaign for Real Beauty has seen Dove maintain its position as the leading cleansing brand. At a cost of between €10 and €20 million, the 2004 European 'Real Curves' campaign, which targeted women in their thirties, exceeded expectations by growing market share in the six largest markets by 13.5 per cent. In the USA, Dove sales reportedly logged double digit growth rates (Gogoi 2005). It seems that the Campaign for Real Beauty also provided highly valued leadership and professional development opportunities for a substantial number of women creatives and brand managers in the O&M and Dove networks.

Gender and creative labour

The Neil French incident and the two Unilever case studies suggest that the attitudes of advertisers and agency principles can unnecessarily constrain the use of creative approaches in advertising to women. Employment practices and work cultures in advertising can also act as a deterrent to women pursuing creative careers, thus diluting the pool of creative human resources that the industry can draw on in its efforts to communicate with women. When viewed in total, the participation rates of women in advertising generally seem equitable. However, this obscures the existence of entrenched patterns of 'vertical and horizontal gender segregation' (Nixon 2003: 96) in industry employment patterns. So, for example, while the Institute of Practitioners in Advertising (IPA) reported that 49.6 per cent of UK agency employees were women in 2003, only 11 per cent of agency chairs, CEOs and managing directors were female (IPA 2004: 5). This was a 2 per cent improvement on the participation rates of women in the senior ranks of the industry in 2000 (Nixon 2003). However, the participation of women in creative advertising appears to have been in decline for a number of years. In 2000 the IPA reported that only 18 per cent of women held creative positions in agencies. The IPA did not report on this breakdown in its subsequent 2003 census. During the 1980s and 1990s women in American agencies gained increased access to more media and account management positions but 'lost ground in creative departments', accounting for an estimated 24 per cent of creative positions in 1997

(Maxwell 2003). Similar patterns are also apparent in Australian agencies. Between 2004 and 2005, the proportion of women in creative positions actually declined from 26 to 23 per cent (AFA *c.*2005). Prospects for advancement were also better for women in areas such as account management than in creative direction. According to the Advertising Federation of Australia, 25 per cent of senior management were women in 2005, compared with 19.4 per cent in 2004. However, the percentage of females occupying senior positions as Creative Directors also declined in the same period, from 9 to 6 per cent.

Important insights on how these inequities have arisen and are maintained in agency work cultures have come, in recent years, from cultural studies. Because it sits at the intersection of culture and economy, creative advertising has been an obvious and very rich site for exploring the role of culture in economic life using the ethnographic methods and sub-cultural analytical techniques of cultural studies. In his analysis of the informal cultures and subjective identities of key practitioners associated with the rise of creative advertising in the UK in the 1990s, Sean Nixon makes a number of important observations about the ways in which creative advertising practice has been simultaneously gendered and made commercially productive (Nixon 2003). He finds that the discourse of creativity shared by creatives and management actively supported the prevailing laddish culture of creative departments. Young men were taken to be the wellsprings of vast, irrepressible reserves of creative energy. Consequently, these were often hostile and difficult workplaces for women creatives. Managers justified the absence of women from their creative departments on the grounds that women's presence had the effect of forcing 'the young male creatives to grow up and thus erode the essential juvenility that was crucial to performing the roles of art director and copywriter' (Nixon 2003: 105). Frank Mort previously traced this development to elite definitions of creativity that made their way from art schools into British advertising in the 1980s.

> In the 1980s the enobled status of the creative team was made possible by the demand for a different style of advertising, which promised added value through what was perceived to be a more sophisticated approach to commercial communications. Inside the firm, agency directors also drew on elite definitions of creativity, originating in fine art, in order to bolster their claims to rank. Like the style leaders, advertising professionals claimed an aesthetic pedigree.
>
> (Mort 1996: 100)

These were the people who saw the 'division between advertising and art as a false dichotomy' (Mort 1996: 101) and who argued that advertising was the art form of late capitalism. They resisted work practices that attempted to commodify creative labour and, in the process, reproduced the pre-exiting cultural and structural barriers that had previously largely limited the possibilities of artistic genius to men. The confluence of this new wave of creative advertising with the globalization of capital and the global restructuring of advertising from the 1980s and throughout the 1990s, also served to reinforce these assumptions. During this period, industry deregulation eroded the commission system of remuneration. In response, media buyers split from advertising agencies to establish new specialist agencies. This left the creative agencies in need of new revenue models and intensified the pressures on them to extract greater value from their creative resources. The male domination of creative advertising work cultures intensified in this time. This is the reality reflected in the low participation rates of women. As one highly placed industry executive commented anonymously,

> women hate it. They are scared stiff of it. It's not like anything they know of performance-based culture. It is performance-based only in that if you don't have very good ideas on a regular basis . . . you don't have a job for long. Successful creative teams are greatly valued by agencies and therefore behaviour is tolerated that would not be tolerated elsewhere.

Significantly, though, Nixon found that the gendered notions of creativity and assumptions about appropriate management practices embedded in creative advertising discourse and agency practices were in fact widespread throughout many 'new' economy sectors. He associated it with a paradigmatic shift in patterns and performances of work in Western economies. In short, symbol creators are loosely controlled, relative to the degree of control exercised over distribution. This finding is consistent with a more general pattern of the organization of the 'copyright' and 'creative' industries (Hesmondhalgh 2002: 21ff.). In other words, the challenges of managing creative labour are not particular to advertising. As creativity has come into focus over the past decade as the source of competitive advantage to firms across many service sectors, the question of how best to manage creative workforces has emerged as a widespread one, particularly in those industries which rely heavily on creative inputs (for example, Davis and Scase 2000). The exclusionary consequences of those employment practices and work cultures that presume creativity to be a masculine characteristic have also begun to come to the critical attention of sociologists and cultural studies academics (for example, Gill 2002).

Creative advertising in the global era

Advertising is one of the major creative industries, not only because of its primary role in marketing but also because of its secondary economic impact. It is the major revenue source for many other creative industries, including the print and broadcast media and, as discussed throughout this book, new media. As the Axe/Lynx and Dove case studies demonstrate, advertising is a major cultural resource. While the masculine coding of creativity accounts, at least in part, for low participation rates of women in creative roles in advertising, and for broader failures of creative advertising in respect of female markets, it is also the case that globalization has had profound consequences for these developments. This can be accessed through a brief review of the context in which present gender codes of creativity in advertising arose.

As outlined in the previous chapter, two broad traditions have evolved in the modern history of advertising and anchor theoretical understandings of advertising techniques and their social and economic effects. In the informational tradition, advertising makes claims about the reasons why consumers should acquire something. Numerous techniques have evolved in this tradition, including the 'hard-sell', which draws attention to the unique selling points of a product (Leiss *et al.* 1997: 149ff.). In this tradition, the consumer is assumed to be a stable and reasonable subject whose behaviour can be predicted through the application of market research informed by scientific method. This contrasts with the creative advertising tradition in which imagery prevails. This tradition takes a more persuasive, soft-sell approach in advertising appeals. It has come to emphasize design, desire, fashion, lifestyle and the multifaceted possibilities that consumption opens up for constructing and expressing individual identity. It draws heavily upon intuitive and experiential knowledge of consumers and the wider social and cultural contexts of consumption.

This division of the field along informational and creative lines at times seems quite arbitrary, if not unstable. Both approaches are subject to constant innovation and are not necessarily clearly identifiable as one or the other with the passage of time. For example, in his time, David Ogilvy led numerous highly creative branding campaigns, but distanced himself from later creative trends, preferring to take his lead from the 'reason why' school at the heart of direct response techniques (Ogilvy 2004). Indeed, the stamp of the O&M house style was still clearly apparent in the Campaign for Real Beauty and its heavy reliance on market research as the basis for creative action. In the light of subsequent developments in creative advertising, Ogilvy's achievements now seem more closely aligned with an information-based model of consumer behaviour. As consumer behaviour academic and anthropologist Grant McCracken observes, this persists as a prevailing paradigm in much consumer research and,

> conceives of the consumer as someone who is information centred, someone constantly seeking out and manipulating information in order to make choices between consumer goods and services.
>
> (McCracken 2005: 165)

The range of approaches to advertising is probably more usefully thought of as a continuum, with information-centred notions of the consumer at one end and meaning-centred ones at the other. Although there is evidence that meaning-centred approaches have been practised throughout the history of advertising, and cultural studies has always recognized the centrality of meaning in theories of consumption, it is only in the past decade or so that these approaches have begun to be formally theorized at the intersection of marketing and cultural anthropology. Here, McCracken and others argue that advertising is used by consumers in quite a different manner to that presumed by the information-oriented model.

> Consumers are looking for something they can use in their constructions of new versions of the self, the family, a community. They are seeking not meaning with a capital 'M', the existential notion of the term. They are looking for small meanings, concepts of what it is to be a parent, concepts of what a child is and what a child is becoming, concepts of what it is to be a member of a community and a country. These are our preoccupations in a time and place that has given the individual liberties in matters of self-definition. . . . One of our sources of instruction and experimentation here is the advertisement. When the consumer looks at ads, he or she is looking for symbolic resources, new ideas and better concrete versions of old ideas with which to advance the project.
>
> (McCracken 2005: 165)

In short, creative advertising puts a greater emphasis on motivation and meaning than on market research. Meaning-centred approaches to advertising, which invited increased reliance on imagery and visual culture, also benefited from twentieth century developments in broadcast media, especially the dispersion of television as a new mass medium of information and entertainment. Also, in the post-World War II period, advances in creative approaches to advertising were enhanced by insights from psychiatry, psychology and the social sciences into the emotional motivations underpinning consumer choices and buying decisions (Packard 1960: 17–25).

Some advertising historians have argued that the history of advertising has been governed by alternating cycles of informational and creative advertising (for example, Fox 1997). These cycles are strongly influenced by economic conditions. So, for example, advertisers are more willing to experiment with creative approaches in periods of sustained growth, but retreat to more risk-averse informational methods in periods of economic contraction. Other historians seek a more nuanced position, observing instead that both styles have 'come in and out of favour with different agencies at different times, for different classes of product, or with different types of audiences' and, since the 1980s, have even been blended within ads and ad campaigns (Leiss *et al.* 1997, 149ff.). Despite their uneasy co-existence, and the many slippages between them, these two traditions have served to provide an important means of differentiation between agencies in a highly competitive industry. Importantly, and of particular interest here, the differing approaches to understanding consumers and consumption have had different consequences for industry and agency culture and politics. For example, when advertiser demand for creative advertising is strong, advertising creatives can wield a lot of influence. When demand for more informational approaches is strong, account managers tend to call the shots.

There is also more than a hint of a trans-Atlantic rivalry in the meta-conversation about the informational/creative dichotomization of advertising history. This dates from the boom period of the 1980s when the innovations of many newly established British creative advertising agencies were claimed as the distinguishing features of globally significant trends in advertising. Meaning-centred approaches to understanding consumers and consumption provided the foundations of success in the British creative turn. However, in this period, the meaning of creativity expanded to describe a new way of conducting the business of advertising. Emblematic of the influence of this shift in British creative agencies was Saatchi & Saatchi, which broke with numerous conventions of advertising business. Building on its early success with breakthrough creative campaigns, Saatchi & Saatchi pursued a growth strategy that re-engineered the business of advertising in a number of profound ways in a very short period.

Saatchi & Saatchi was an early adopter of the philosophy of globalization as advanced by Harvard business professor and Saatchi mentor, Theodore Levitt (Levitt 1983). This argued the case for the global standardization of products and marketing on the grounds that the segmentation of consumer markets could be achieved on a global scale. It went against the grain of industry wisdom of the time. Although already highly internationalized, industry practices tended to favour more localized campaign approaches. Levitt's philosophy of globalization informed marketing strategies for swiftly responding to the opportunities presented in rapidly emerging consumer markets, which at the time focused on Eastern Europe (Arens 2002: 36). Its logic was also applied to the business of advertising itself. Rather than follow the established industry growth path of expansion through new billings, Saatchi & Saatchi opted for an aggressive acquisitions programme on a scale not seen before in advertising. This growth strategy meant that agencies could offer globalizing corporate clients bundled and, ultimately, integrated services 'in an age of procurement' (quoted in Tannos 2003). The global consolidation of advertising sparked by Saatchi & Saatchi extended into all marketing disciplines, including direct marketing, sales promotion, design and public relations. Even the way that

Saatchi & Saatchi funded its own expansion was unprecedented. Agencies had started publicly listing in the 1960s, a development that also significantly changed agency culture (Cappo 2003). Saatchi & Saatchi played this development to the firm's advantage, and used the novel instrument of stock options to finance their programme of rapid expansion. As advertising historian Stephen Fox explains,

> Saatchi offered new stock at discount prices to existing shareholders. Cash for corporate hunting thus came without immediate debt, without even a requirement to disclose intentions to the public, while shareholders as supporters of the enterprise enjoyed pre-emptive rights to bargain stocks. Any unsold shares then went to outside investors at higher prices. This method provided bushels of short-term cash – at the dangerous expense of long-term vision and responsibilities. It was very much a young man's gambit, redoubled by the heady expansionist fervour of the business world of the 1980s.
>
> (Fox 1997: xiv)

In the space of 15 years, Saatchi & Saatchi became the largest holding company in the world before WPP, another new mega-group and the brainchild of former Saatchi & Saatchi finance director Martin Sorrell, usurped its position. Armand Mattelart describes this period, in which global holding companies emerged to challenge the pre-eminence of American agencies for the first time as the 'third wave' in the internationalization of advertising. In this scheme of advertising history, the first wave of internationalization extended from the end of the nineteenth century to the period between World War I and World War II. It was imperial to the extent that it closely followed the international expansion of the 'great' American enterprises (Mattelart 2002: 3). The second wave gained momentum after World War II. It was pursued with a conviction that the broader strategic interests of the USA were served by international advertising networks. They 'were not simply new promotional circuits for industrial and commercial products, but also networks of cultural and political influence' (Mattelart 2002: 32). In the third wave of internationalization, agencies became highly globally networked and 'deeply marked by the process of interpenetration of firms and markets' (Mattelart 2002: 36). Global standardization of digital communication systems and the harmonization of rules of access to media through mechanisms such as trade agreements were also symptomatic of the wider transformative influences of globalization (Mattelart 2002: 86).

Importantly, the success of Saatchi & Saatchi in rapidly articulating advertising services to a changing global economic order followed from earlier successes in creative advertising. As Frank Mort has argued, Saatchi & Saatchi built its competitive advantage from 'an innovative, youthful and, above all, imaginative approach to promotional culture' (Mort 1996: 93). This marked a wider shift in British creative advertising that perceived investments in knowledge as the new sources of added value and wealth creation. It coincided with similar changes in entrepreneurial strategy taking shape in high technology industries. The young social science and humanities graduates who entered British advertising at this time brought with them new theoretical perspectives on consumer culture from which a more meaning-centred toolkit of predictive market research was built. This included 'semiotic analysis and linguistic deconstruction, together with up-to-date thinking about the structures of postmodern or postindustrial society' (Mort 1996: 103). In this context, the concept of creativity came to signify a shift 'in what might be termed the epistemologies of the consumer process' (Mort 1996: 103). As illustrated by the Lynx/Axe case, these new orientations to consumer research provided extremely productive means for developing new markets, extending the reach of consumer capitalism in mature consumer societies.

A major principle problem for marketing since World War II has been stimulating demand in societies where most people with the capacity to purchase already have everything they need. John Hegarty, the founding partner of another very influential third wave creative agency, BBH (the agency that brought us the Axe/ Lynx Effect), says image provided 'the only possible answer' to this problem.

> Nowadays products work and they tend to be more or else equal, so you buy what you believe is the brand that you should be seen with. So really we've entered the world of fashion in which creativity and innovative thinking are paramount.
>
> (quoted in Benady 2005)

By the 1980s, choices had proliferated in all consumer categories, including media, where niche media were in the ascendancy. Creative advertising proved that effective product differentiation based on branding required more meaning-centred foundations than either hard or soft sell 'reason why' approaches could support. In the third wave of advertising, many new creative agencies established themselves as *rapporteurs* in a global dialogue between informationalizing capitalism and popular culture. Advertising creatives, along with their counterparts in other parts of the marketing and media complex, emerged as key mediators of consumer capitalism, and were remarkably successful in establishing new markets, especially in youth segments. The extent to which the particular gendering of creativity that arose in the third wave of internationalization can be impressed on the co-evolutionary paths of advertising and new media is, however, a more open question.

Gender and conversational media

Despite its military origins and its enabling capacity for all sorts of new cultural formations – including highly misogynistic ones – the internet is far from being coded as a predominantly masculine domain. Feminist commentators have been quick to note the feminine qualities of its core affordances (Spender 1995; Van Zoonen 2002). As a medium of consensus, cooperation, conversation and social networking, parallels have been drawn between the internet and the earlier coding of intrinsic uses of telephone-based communication as feminine. This is one way in which the internet has been reclaimed as an expression of femininity. Liesbet van Zoonen also observes that in claiming the internet to be a woman's medium many feminist authors, 'find themselves in an unexpected and unsolicited alliance with internet marketing researchers', for whom the internet provides unprecedented opportunities to reach women (Van Zoonen 2002: 10). Van Zoonen is herself more circumspect. Her own research suggests that although domestication of the networked personal computer has made the internet more accessible to women, gender power relations still shape internet usage in the home. However, the trend to individualization of media devices and customization of services could erode and ultimately disconnect gender-based power relations from the ongoing social shaping of media.

There can be little doubt that advertising, along with media and communications industries, has contributed to the increased visibility of women and domestic social space in the course of the twentieth century (Peiss 1996). This visibility has been controversial but important in the wider legitimation of women in the political and economic life of many Western societies. However, it is not enough that modern women are seen; there is an ongoing need for women to participate in their own imaging. Networked do-it-yourself media, such as blogs, can and do support precisely these developments.

Thus, three related tensions emerge for advertising from the particular gendering of creativity considered here. First, the creative approach to advertising has generated important new knowledge about male consumers. This has been very successfully applied in the development of new markets for established product categories, including the category of cosmetics and beauty, considered here. Second, similar creative success in relation to female consumers would require the acquisition and mobilization of equivalent culturally-based understandings of women consumers, most usually embodied in the people selected to work in and lead creative departments. It requires a re-coding of creativity in advertising as both masculine and feminine. However, the short-term costs and risks associated with the knock-on effects that these sorts of changes would have on advertising creative work practices appear to be more than many parts of the industry are presently willing to bear. Nevertheless, in a media environment where end-users exercise control over instant, global conversation, advertisers face serious and unanticipated consequences for failures of communication with consumers. Advertising has a demonstrable, sophisticated, creative conversational capacity, but it also has important limits, and the will to address these limits in relation to women is still in contention.

Chapter 4

Mobilizing the local

Advertising and cell phone industries in China

The cell phone has been widely adopted as the communications medium of choice in many parts of the world and stimulated the development of significant new consumer cultures and economies (for example, Rheingold 2002; Goggin 2006). In the People's Republic of China, advertising is deeply implicated in this development. The rebirth of advertising and advertising-supported media in the world's most populous country have facilitated China's development as the world's largest mobile communications market. The interests of advertisers and government are important influences on the patterns of ongoing diffusion and development for cell phones and services, but underlying these factors is unprecedented consumer demand for conversational media. The example of contemporary China also presents an opportunity to recalibrate some observations made by critics and advocates alike about the restlessness of advertising. For example, advertising, and its attendant problems of clutter and environmental degradation, is seen as emblematic of the expansionary imperative of monopoly capitalism (McAllister 1996; Klein 2000; Turner 1965: 106; Ogilvy 2004: 156). It simultaneously serves as an index of the colonization of public space and culture by commercial interests, and of freedom and the spread of liberal democracy (McAllister 1996; Arens 2002).

Since the communist government of the People's Republic of China first embarked on a programme of economic modernization in the late 1970s, foreign comprehension of China has tended to oscillate between Cold War inspired anxieties about the influence of state ideology and enchantment with the sheer size of the developing Chinese consumer society (Keane and Spurgeon 2005). Reform has introduced a variety of disruptive factors that neither position can adequately accommodate. Chinese media scholars have argued that the impact of the reform process on Chinese media and communications requires a frame of understanding that lies somewhere between these poles (Donald *et al*. 2002: 6). Reform has facilitated the dispersal of central government control to emergent sites of political and economic power, including the 32 provinces, special economic regions and so-called autonomous regions of China, as well as to the state-owned media and communications enterprises. An international orientation in public policy accompanied the shift to a market economy. Chinese bureaucrats and business people look to other parts of Asia, especially Singapore and Malaysia, for trade opportunities as well as models of media, while Chinese consumers monitor the media and popular cultural trends of places such as Hong Kong, Japan, Korea and Taiwan. China's re-entry into the world economy, formally recognized in 2001 when it qualified for World Trade Organization (WTO) membership, increased certainty in trade and investment with China, but also introduced new sources of uncertainty into Chinese politics, economy and civil society.

China has rehabilitated both advertising and consumption as instruments of national economic renewal and global integration. Advertising is now highly valued by the central government for what it can contribute to the mission of economic renewal. This includes its capacity to help strengthen the international competitiveness and export orientation of 'national champions', Chinese brands that can compete locally and abroad with global brands (Nolan 2001). The role of advertising in the rapid movement of high-performing Chinese brands, from local to global market orientation, is illustrated in the second part of this chapter with a case study of the Bird brand of Chinese cell phones. As a result of astute local marketing and advertising, the Bird brand quickly built a significant national share of the handset market. Within three years of entering the market, Bird had displaced global brands such as Motorola and Nokia, and for a time was the top-selling handset brand in China. Bird's horizons also expanded to include the rapid development of export markets.

In the process of developing an export orientation, Chinese firms have incorporated global advertising into their marketing repertoire. While transnational advertisers may have pioneered the global advertising appeal as a cost-effective way of rapidly building brand awareness in new national markets, it is by no means the exclusive preserve of transnational advertisers. Indeed, advertising has been assigned a strategically important responsibility to support the movement of Chinese manufacturing and services industries up the value chain of wealth creation. This movement has been described as the difference between 'made in China' and 'created in China' (Keane 2007). It is a pattern of economic development that other Asian economies share, notably Hong Kong, Japan, Korea, Taiwan and Singapore, and which others, in addition to China, seek to emulate.

Advertising, media and consumer culture are being used quite explicitly to hasten the modernization and internationalization of the Chinese economy and its society. Chinese authorities and consumers alike are important agents in the formation of markets, although how this agency might be framed is a matter of contention. The motivations of Chinese government authorities in engineering the development of the world's largest consumer society are not usefully understood as those of willing collaborators in the geopolitical expansion of capital, as the logic of critical political economies of advertising might otherwise suggest. Nor does the priority status of markets in contemporary Chinese politics offer an adequate basis for understanding the astounding growth of either advertising or the new media of mobile communications. As Michael Schudson has observed of consumer culture more generally, demand for material goods is consumer-led (Schudson 1993: 249). An active conception of engaged consumers is required, but it cannot be limited to a rational basis for demand. An 'aesthetic economy' also springs from different ways of life (Negus 2002), not just those that might be characteristically aristocratic or bourgeois.

The success of Chinese and international handset brands occurred against a backdrop of 'an astounding and unforeseen phenomenon', the rapid adoption of mobile communications in China (MFC Insight 2003: 2.2). The number of Chinese with access to any kind of telephone service has dramatically increased in the past decade from less than one in ten to five in ten people, in part due to the development of mobile communications. Over half of the telephone connections in China are mobile, and the actual numbers involved dwarf those of any other national market. With more than 350 million connections, China is the largest cell phone market in the world. Service and infrastructure quality, availability and handset aesthetics have been important considerations in consumer choices. The affordability of handsets and services, as well as the knowledge-based capacity of users to find relevant applications for mobile communications, are also important factors that shape patterns and rates of adoption. The growth of mobile communications has had a major impact on the Chinese telecommunications industry and in society more generally, and has been driven by extraordinary levels of demand for access to the multifaceted benefits that accrue to users. These benefits are not limited to the values of modern consumerism, advertising's stock in trade; they also include the affordances of a new platform of conversational interaction.

Advertising and media reform in China

China's first encounter with consumer culture was in the 1920s and 1930s, the period between the two World Wars, when the port city of Shanghai was a thriving centre of international trade and commerce. Advertising was one of many service industries to prosper in this period. By the time the communists took power in 1949 there were about 100 advertising agencies in Shanghai, but this number quickly diminished as the role of advertising changed. In the command economies of China and the USSR, the role of advertising in marketing was highly constrained, and was usually limited to serving production cycles in specified ways. It was an inventory management tool, used to address problems of over-production and obsolescence, or to move seasonal produce that could not be stored (Frith and Meuller 2003: 66–8). Market competition was limited in these state-controlled economies. In China's case, the need for advertising was 'virtually eliminated' (Chang *et al.* 2003: 458). Socialist aesthetics saw advertising banished from the urban environment and replaced by other forms of state-sanctioned publicity that reflected the values and ideology of the Chinese state. This function of advertising is evident in the etymology of the Chinese verb for propagandizing (*xuanchuan*: literally, to disseminate), which still connotes the meaning: to advertise. By 1956, the year that capitalism was officially abolished in China, all of Shanghai's advertising agencies had been consolidated in the state-owned Shanghai Advertising Corporation, later renamed the Shanghai Fine Arts Corporation in the Cultural Revolution (Wang 2003).

China's current encounter with global consumer culture began in the late 1970s, following Mao's death and Deng Xiaoping's pragmatic 'open-door' initiative. This ended China's extended period of international isolation. It re-established the flow of foreign capital to China that triggered an uneven renewal of commercial culture and, with it, the rebirth of advertising. Advertising has since become 'the fastest developing industry' in China (Zhao 1998: 55). The Japanese-based agency, Dentsu, was first to establish a presence in China in 1979 – the year that Chinese media began accepting advertising again – and pursued an aggressive programme of Japanese brand awareness in metropolitan and national Chinese media. By 1981 no less than five multinational agencies had established joint ventures or partnerships with local companies, and many others followed. Throughout the 1980s, the surging consumer economies of former Soviet Bloc countries and other parts of Asia fuelled the global consolidation of the international advertising industry. The incursion of privately owned, commercial media into these same markets occurred in this period of rapid global expansion.

China's own processes of media commercialization and partial privatization intensified in 1992, following National Party Congress endorsement of measures intended to speed up economic reform. As government funding was reduced and withdrawn from all but those print and broadcast media outlets of the greatest strategic interest to the ruling Communist Party, media across China were compelled to turn to advertising in order to survive. Along with various other service industries, media and communications were progressively opened up to private and foreign investment. Economic reform alleviated government inability to invest in media, a problem compounded by growing consumer demand for new services. Publishers and broadcasters either began to meet requirements for funding autonomy by diversifying revenue streams and sources of investment capital, or they failed. In fact, the number of media outlets grew exponentially from this time. In the mid-1990s, it was estimated that a new newspaper was opening in China every one and a half days (Zhao 1998: 57).

Advertising quickly became a major source of income for Chinese media. Already extremely powerful, the influence of state-owned media holding companies has extended into advertising, with most establishing agencies to manage their own inventory and allied production services. The number of agencies grew from about 1,000 in 1981 to 31,000 in 1993, to 57,000 in 1997, and then 89,000 in 2002 (CAA 2003). The number of employees grew from fewer than 20,000 in the early 1980s to half a million in the mid-1990s and reached 756,000 in 2002. With an average annual growth rate of 20 per cent, the Chinese advertising market is projected to be second only to the United States by 2010 (Chan *et al*. 2003: 470).

Medicines and food have been the two dominant categories of advertising expenditure since advertising recommenced in 1979, reflecting China's developing economy status (Howkins 2001: 85). Although goods and services that address basic needs continue to be the most important categories of consumer and advertising expenditure, these patterns are also changing. There have been significant increases in areas such as real estate, cars, household electrical appliances and a range of services that include medical, travel and communication (Huang and Chen 2004), developments consistent with the consumption trends of a growing middle class.

In his analysis of Chinese consumer movements, Karl Gerth argues that there is a deep and continuous connection between Chinese nationalism and consumption that runs across the twentieth century. The strength of popular anti-colonial sentiment contributes, at least in part, to an understanding of 'the speed, thoroughness, and popular acceptance' of the Communist Party's takeover of the state (Gerth 2003: 366). The communist command economy, Gerth argues, is the legacy of China's colonial history. A deep residual ambivalence about foreign capital persists, and it is strategically ameliorated by the Chinese government's present promotion of the virtues of a consumer-led economy on national interest grounds. In many respects, the present strategic value of advertising to the Chinese Communist Party corresponds with that which has previously been associated with the strategic value accorded to advertising by US governments (Schudson 1993: 219). It is tacitly prized as the medium for communicating and promulgating values of consumerism.

The continuity between Chinese nationalism and consumption is also apparent in the contemporary national vision of an internationally competitive Chinese advertising industry that will support the development and export orientation of other internationally competitive Chinese brands. China is not content with being the world's factory, only competitive in the area of unskilled labour, but has ambitions to compete in knowledge-intensive manufacturing and service industries, and has implemented capacity-building strategies to support this end. Cooperative ventures with American multinational advertising agencies, in particular, have been enormously important to the re-construction of advertising in China. With a reputation for producing internationally sought-after industry professionals (Mattelart 2002: 33), these agencies were encouraged to establish presences in China because their workplace-based education and training practices were highly valued as human capital development and knowledge transfer processes. Gilbert Yang, CEO of the Shanghai Advertising Association, Shanghai AdBay, estimates that of the 4,000 or so Chinese advertising professionals trained by international agencies in the 1990s only about one-third remain with them. Approximately one-third moved on to become media managers and the remaining third struck out as independents to build their own agencies (Yang, interview, 2004).

International advertising agencies are also valued because they are an important part of the 'soft infrastructure' that is necessary to facilitating international investment (Keane and Spurgeon 2004: 106). The social networks of global advertising agencies and their clients are an important and effective interface with Chinese *guangxi* – the complex relations of informal networks of social connection, obligation and favour – that underpin Chinese business culture and society in general. Gilbert Yang attributes this to the fact that advertising is, ultimately, a 'people business'. Failure to attend to the soft infrastructure of relationship-building that *guangxi* demands is often a major contributing factor for international companies failing to get traction in China. Good *guangxi* is vital to establishing a Chinese presence because the legal status of national and local markets in geographically diffuse economic reform policy processes is often unclear. This is especially the case for media investments. Global and international advertisers generally value the *guangxi* that local branches of international agencies have been able to develop, not just their expertise in defining, targeting and communicating with desirable consumer markets, or in managing the challenges of cross-cultural communication and translation.

However, levels of foreign advertiser confidence in Chinese markets are also highly variable and volatile. The difficulty that Chinese media encounter in attracting foreign advertiser interest illustrates this point well. Foreign advertisers accounted for about 40 per cent of total advertising expenditure in China in 2002. This was a 'considerable drop' on figures for previous years (Huang and Chen 2004). This reduction in foreign advertising expenditure coincided with the worldwide contraction in advertising, but factors specific to Chinese media also exacerbated uncertainty about the Chinese media and advertising markets. These included the enforcement of stricter consumer protection requirements in certain consumer goods categories, most notably in medicines. The bigger brake on foreign advertiser confidence, however, arose from problems with the reliability of media consumer metrics. Investment in credible independent circulation and readership data for local print media (as distinct from national and international newspaper and magazine titles) has not kept pace with the growth of media outlets. Foreign advertisers are reluctant to make use of the rapidly segmenting local media ecology in the absence of reliable intelligence about it. Establishing a reliable auditing system that covers all of China is a major logistical challenge and, curiously, does not appear to be a high priority for local media. These factors put immense upward pressure on the value of those media that are performing well. Consequently, media such as the national China Central Television (CCTV) are reputed to be some of the most expensive in the world (Yang, interview, 2004).

The Chinese advertising industry has tended to bifurcate along local and national/international lines. Figure 4.1 shows that foreign joint venture agencies generally provide a full range of services to global brands. They also principally use international and national media to reach consumers in the comparatively wealthy urban centres of Beijing, Shanghai and Guangzhou, the so-called 'Tier 1' cities of China. Local Chinese agencies often provide a far more limited range of services for local brands. Many are state-owned enterprises in non-media services developing new revenue streams. For example, a large number of Chinese advertising agencies are divisions of local public transport authorities keen to develop and grow outdoor advertising clients. Where local agencies do compete in the provi-

Full service

International agencies
(e.g. Dentsu, Ogilvy & Mather, JWT, etc.)
All global holding companies represented in China

Chinese agencies
(e.g. PCBP)
Very few

Suppliers
(e.g. production services, etc.)
High end tends to go offshore. Many Chinese suppliers at the low to medium end

Media-owned agencies
(e.g. outdoor, print, broadcast, etc.)
Tens of thousands of Chinese agencies plan/sell/provide creative services for their own inventory

Specialized services

Figure 4.1 Structure of the Chinese advertising industry

sion of other services they may do so at less than cost, undercutting full service agencies.

Until they were abolished recently, tiered rate cards meant that global advertisers were systematically charged more than local advertisers for the same media. Heavy rate card discounting in *guangxi* networks has also favoured the local industry in the short term, but is unsustainable in the medium to long term (Keane and Spurgeon 2004: 106). These sorts of practices have been identified as discriminatory, and have come under pressure in the wake of China's accession to the World Trade Organization (WTO) in 2001. As part of the WTO process, China made commitments on the regulation of trade in various service industry sectors, including advertising. Concessions included opening up to direct foreign investment in advertising agencies. Full foreign ownership of agencies has been permitted since 2005.

The far-reaching and irreversible impact of WTO accession on China's key economic infrastructure has been welcomed by the central government as a 'wrecking ball' that will stimulate economic growth (Keane and Spurgeon 2004: 108). This analogy refers to what Joseph Schumpeter famously identified as the 'creative destruction' of capitalism, the driving force of its seemingly perpetual reinvention. Through the WTO, the Chinese central government gains access to this force without having to concede regulatory control over key infrastructure and institutions, including media and communications. Media and advertising industries do not generally escape government control as a result of WTO accession. However, government regulation, and the terms and conditions of doing business with China, does have to be made explicit. The multilateral framework requires regulatory transparency, and provides mechanisms for negotiated solutions to free trade disputes. WTO critics argue that the greatest weakness of this approach to fostering the global economy is that it does not distinguish between free trade and fair trade, and does not account for the massive global inequities that this failure produces. China's accession to the WTO could be read as a triumph of global capitalism. It could also be an acknowledgement of China's significance as an emerging geopolitical centre of gravity in the global economy. With its modern history of anti-imperialist, socialist revolution, and its demographic critical mass, China may yet emerge on the world stage as a rule-maker rather than a rule-taker in a range of trade-related matters, including advertising services.

In the early years of reform, the advertising industry was subject to rules enforced by various government agencies, including the very powerful State Administration for Industry and Commerce (SAIC). A legislative basis for advertising regulation was not put in place until the mid-1990s with the promulgation of the Advertising Law of 1995 (Chang *et al.* 2003). This formalized a complex web of dispersed advertising governance, a legacy of the command economy and the

Chinese Marxist critique of advertising. When compared with many other countries, advertising in China seems to be 'very heavily regulated' (Frith and Meuller 2003: 86). This outward appearance belies a complex reality. Responsibility for content regulation is dispersed to advertising agencies and media organizations, who administer a prior approval process to which all ads are submitted. In practice, this process can look more like an indirect tax on advertising disguised as content regulation. So, although advertising and media content continue to be heavily regulated and are potentially subject to centralized control, various factors, including the local politics of these industries and the dispersed responsibility for content regulation, mean that rules might be interpreted differently in different provinces, and compliance may not always be achieved, or consistently achieved. Nevertheless, international market analysts perceive Chinese advertising laws and regulations to be 'very protective of consumer interests' (Chang *et al.* 2003: 461–3). A registration scheme for advertising professionals, similar to accreditation schemes for professionals such as chartered accountants, was being seriously considered at the time of writing as a way of providing enforceable, distributed industry self-regulation. If implemented, this scheme would tighten the accountability of advertising agencies by assigning the liability for the accuracy, appropriateness and compliance of advertising with specified advertising rules to accredited professionals within advertising agencies and media organizations (Yang, interview, 2004).

In spite of state control, growth in Chinese media and consumer markets has been both rapid and chaotic. Advertising, both local and international, has played an important role in facilitating the commercialization and growth of Chinese media and the development of consumerism in China. This transformation is being encouraged from the highest levels of Chinese political authority. Investors who seek fortunes in the developing Chinese consumer markets are also energetically embracing it. As the following case of the cell phone handset industry indicates, consumer markets are also consumer-driven.

Marketing cell phones in China

The growth rate of Chinese consumer markets for cell phones has taken many observers by surprise. Without wishing to overstate the impact of the cell phone in ameliorating the so-called 'digital divide' (Hill and Dhanda 2002) and taken in the context of generic growth factors associated with domestic economic reform, this technology has allowed Chinese consumers to bypass fixed line service connection costs and queues and leapfrog into the globalizing networked society. In a very short period of time, China has emerged as both the global centre of cell phone manufacturing and the world's largest consumer market for cell phone handsets and services.

Many features of the Chinese cell phone market are common the world over, including the dominance of global brands such as Motorola (USA), Nokia (Finland), Siemens (Germany) and Samsung (Korea). There are also distinctive local features which, due to the sheer size and complexity of the Chinese market, have significant global impacts. One of these features is the large number of local Chinese handset manufacturers. The interplay of local business practices with government policy ambitions to foster export-oriented 'national champions' means that local Chinese manufacturers are highly resistant to market rationalization pressures. Consequently, over 40 local and international brands tout hundreds of handset models in a highly competitive and crowded market (ABC 2004). Competition for market share is often based on price rather than brand values. While Chinese branded phones have performed well in these circumstances, and now account for up to 40 per cent of total Chinese cell phone sales, this success is not explained away by policy settings which favour local manufacturers undercutting international brands on price alone. The application and localization of marketing communications disciplines are also important influences.

Despite increases in advertising expenditure and a history of Chinese nationalism expressed through consumerism, Chinese brands have not generally enjoyed the same levels of consumer awareness that global brands have in the reform era. However, in some product and service categories, such as mobile communications devices, Chinese brands have begun to close this gap. Exposure to foreign competition has seen Chinese brands increase their competitiveness on quality and price; they can no longer be as predictably read as markers of inferiority, as being unfashionable in a product category dominated by global brands. Government-sponsored 'Buy Chinese' campaigns have also had an impact; and poor translation of foreign brands into the Chinese market has worked in favour of local brands (Zhou and Belk 2004: 72).

Rising consumer awareness of Chinese cell phone brands also indicates the successful local appropriation and application of international advertising and marketing know-how. The marketing and communications capacity that local handset manufacturers, Ningbo Bird and TCL, have developed to reach Chinese consumers is a major factor contributing to the success of these brands. This extends to distribution, retail sales and customer support networks that enable national reach. Attention to marketing logistics beyond the first tier cities distinguishes these companies from global brands and dozens of other local manufacturers. Global brands have also attempted to establish retail networks beyond the major cities, but find the logistics of China's size, as well as its cultural and linguistic diversity, extremely difficult to manage (Rose 2004).

Brands such as Motorola, Nokia and Sony-Ericsson found the Chinese market to be tough going in the early years of the millennium. Motorola established affiliates in China in the 1990s and was the market leader in the handset market until 2002, with Nokia, Ericsson and Siemens also performing well in the big coastal cities of Beijing, Shanghai and Guangzhou. Apparently unencumbered by the need to return money for shareholders, companies like TCL and Ningbo Bird, meanwhile, grew to dominate the lower end market and have since tended to confine the international brands to higher end market niches.

The case of Ningbo Bird (Bird, hereafter) illustrates how localization of international integrated marketing communication theory and practice informed the growth of consumer markets through segmentation and the incorporation of co-adaptive design innovation in cell phone manufacturing processes.[1] Within four years of entering the mobile phone market in 1999, Bird matched and exceeded its major local competitor, TCL, achieving a 10 per cent market share by 2003, with sales exceeding 13 million units. By 2002 Bird claimed it was wholly responsible for designing one in seven of the phones it was manufacturing and selling in China. Bird-branded phones are now shipped to various South East Asian, Indian, Eastern European and Middle Eastern markets. This particular development trajectory reflects the capacity-building strategy that China is pursuing in knowledge-intensive manufacturing and service industries, as well as the importance of marketing and advertising to this mission. Bird's rapid evolution from fabricator to designer and branded exporter occurred in a very short period, but can be periodized into three distinct phases. Phase 1 was the early period of establishment and market entry and relied on Taiwanese advertising 'know how'. Phase 2 – the period from 2000 to 2003 – was the period of brand awareness. Key to this period was the use of market research to build knowledge of culturally and geographically distinctive, fashion-conscious Chinese consumers, and to segment the Chinese market along these lines. Phase 3 – the period from 2004 to the present – is the export orientation phase.

Bird was established in the early 1990s by four young engineers to manufacture Chinese-developed pagers. The English name 'Bird' was apparently chosen because the connotations of a small, fast and unfettered entity appealed to the founders (Rose 2004). So too did the similar-sounding Chinese name *bodao*, which is translated as 'leader in communications'. The company became the leading local brand of Chinese pagers, second only to the US-based electronics manufacturer, Motorola, one of the first communications manufacturers to enter China in the late 1980s. Critical to Bird's success in pagers was the national network of call centres it developed to support the paging service. These also doubled as customer support and retail outlets. This logistical network gave Bird a major advantage when it moved into cell phone manufacturing and marketing.

Bird saw an opportunity to establish itself in cell phone handsets in the late 1990s when French defence communications technology company, Sagem, was looking for a way to enter the Chinese market (Einhorn 2003). Sagem provided the basic components for mobile phones and Bird provided manufacturing, distribution and customer service. Bird went on to establish partnerships with Korean and Taiwanese components manufacturers and designers, and also began to invest in its own handset design R&D. Bird was listed on the Shanghai stock exchange in 2000, the same year that it secured a Chinese government licence to manufacture mobile telephone handsets under its own brand. The state-owned conglomerate, China Putian, was its largest shareholder. While a beneficiary of state investment, Bird differed from most other Chinese mobile handset manufacturers, including its domestic competitor, TCL, in that it was the only one that did not have a history of direct state ownership.

In the first year of marketing handsets under its own brand, Bird relied on advertising developed by a Taiwanese agency to compete with the global brands that dominated the domestic market. This campaign featured a well-known Taiwanese pop star, CoCo Lee. Since 1994, when Hutchison first used celebrity advertising in the Hong Kong cell phone market with outstanding results, celebrity endorsement has been regarded as an effective, though predictable, approach to selling cell phones and services in Asian markets (Ho *et al*. 1997). By the end of 2000 Bird had sold approximately 700,000 handsets. In the Chinese market context – a behemoth of demanding consumers – this performance failed to satisfy Bird, which aimed to improve its position. It did this by changing its marketing and communication strategies.

Bird continued to use CoCo Lee after Phase 1 because Taiwanese popular culture has strong appeal in mainland China, but appointed a mainland full service agency, PCBP, in 2000 to segment Bird's consumer market and develop a range of marketing strategies and advertising appeals to reach a more diversified customer base. PCBP launched Bird to national prominence with a bold, high-profile campaign that integrated sponsorship, product placement and main media advertising. Bird sponsored the Chinese television coverage of the Sydney 2000 Olympic Games. Journalists involved in the live coverage gave Bird handsets to winning Chinese athletes so that they could call home from the winners' dais. All this post-victory activity was incidentally included in live Chinese television coverage and then later re-purposed in advertisements for Bird. This imagery created a very powerful association between Bird and 'national champions', and conveyed the coexistence of traditional Chinese values and global community. According to PCBP Chairman, Wu Xiaobo, this high-impact campaign cost approximately RMB700,000 (Wu, interview, 2004). In addition, the company gave away 100,000 Bird handsets, one of a number of loss-leading strategies that have caused considerable consternation among international market analysts (MFC Insight 2003: 4.2.2).

PCBP is unusual in the Chinese advertising landscape because it is one of a very few domestic full service agencies that takes an integrated approach to marketing communication. Although there are some 70,000 registered advertising agencies in China, most sell media and provide very few high-level specialist services to advertisers. Wu Xiaobo commented that 'most local agencies depend on intuition and not research'. There are relatively few agencies, local or global, that provide an integrated suite of services, including market research, strategy, planning and account management at rates that are affordable for local firms. These factors distinguished PCBP among Chinese advertising agencies and contributed to the knowledge base that Bird used to build market share in Phase 2.

Following the switch to PCBP and the incorporation of systematic market research into communication strategies, Bird achieved exponential growth, increasing to 2.5 million handsets in 2001, and then 7 million in 2002. By 2003 it was vying with TCL for the title of leading local brand. While international brands such as Motorola and Nokia still dominate in international as well as Chinese domestic markets, the Bird success in carving out a 10 per cent market share is now legendary in the Chinese advertising industry. Whereas global brands concentrated on reaching the top end of the Chinese market by promoting handsets with features such as WAP, which could not be supported beyond major metropolitan centres, Bird grew the overall market by developing major new segments in the rapidly urbanizing, so-called second and third tier cities.

Through market research, PCBP was able to capture and deploy local knowledge that Bird could use for both handset casing design and market communication strategies. Bird claims to invest 6 per cent of annual turnover in R&D. Most of this R&D effort has focused on innovations in handset design, in response to consumer demand. According to Wu Xiaobo, designing for, and marketing to, the 'variability' of cell phone fashions has been one of Bird's strengths. Bird produced handsets that appealed to different segments in these developing markets as both *fashionable* and *functional*, while using foreign technology under licence for basic voice and text functionality. The localized application of world-class professional integrated marketing communications standards and services, which built on the logistical assets of the company, played a significant, multifaceted role in the success of the Bird brand.

Each year, PCBP executed three or four campaigns that relied on different types of appeals to communicate Bird product attributes and brand values to different market segments in a variety of media. One campaign employed a 'global' appeal (Zhou and Belk 2004) to convey the luxury status of Bird handsets. Other campaigns emphasized the use of 'advanced' European communications components in two distinct ways: to associate Bird with leading-edge developments in science and technology, and to support youthful appeals to global cosmopolitanism. PCBP also continued to pursue opportunities for high impact product placement.

In considering the factors that contributed to Bird's success in the period following its initial market entry, it is important to be clear about *what Bird did not do*. It did not accept that the Chinese handset market divided neatly into luxury consumer segments that would be dominated by global brands at one end, with Chinese brands confined to no-frills, economy segments at the other. Rather, Bird set out to create a market for a Chinese brand in a luxury product category that Chinese consumers had previously associated with global brands. Global brands also produce economy models to compete for the low end of the market. However, Bird was more successful than the global brands in quickly establishing and growing low-end market share because it responded to the design preferences of this end of the market, and because its retail and service networks reached these consumers. The question that remains for Bird is whether it can develop from its present domestic market base sufficiently so that it can move up the value chain to compete with established global brands at both the economy and luxury ends of the market, domestically and internationally.

The global competitiveness of the mobile telecommunications sector and the size and social significance of the cell phone market in China means that what occurs in the Chinese market has knock-on effects around the world. For example, in 2004 Motorola claimed to have 285 million Chinese mobile phone users compared with 154 million in the USA (Johnsson 2004). Although the Chinese market continues to grow, the rate of return on investment is falling, and this is causing considerable anxiety and bottom-line challenges for international brands that need to maintain a market share in China or risk losing ground globally.

At the same time, intense competition in the domestic market compels Chinese manufacturers to develop export markets because production capacity now exceeds domestic demand. China's mobile phone production capacity reportedly exceeds 100 million units annually, but domestic demand peaked at 80 million units in 2003 (Einhorn 2003). Bird is reported to be the largest exporter of handsets, exporting in excess of 100,000 to South East Asia, India and Russia each month (Clendenin 2004; Rose 2004).

In their study of consumer readings of advertising in contemporary China, Nan Zhou and Russell Belk suggest that, from a consumer perspective, the effective use of a global advertising appeal is not restricted to brands that are sold in multiple national markets (Zhou and Belk 2004). The global advertising appeal can also be thought of as a symbolic repertoire that makes use of registers of local and global differentiation. These are summarized in Table 4.1. Zhou and Belk also estimate that up to three-quarters of Chinese advertisers use a mix of local and global appeals. Bird is an interesting illustration of this observation. However, in its third phase of development, Bird's use of the global appeal reflected the ambition to internationalize the brand. Ads were produced for international as well as domestic consumption. It retained a Chinese face, but it could be located anywhere and was explicitly associated with global meanings of beauty, fashion, luxury and Western know-how.

Bird competes with foreign branded phones on price, design features, availability and after-sales service. In each of these areas it successfully meets the local Chinese market. Whether this success translates into international markets depends on how it responds to a range of factors in the next few years. Such factors include choices about how it meets the preferences of a maturing domestic market; how third generation (3G) mobile technology and services develop in China, including how issues associated with the management of intellectual property rights for 3G communication protocols are addressed; how Chinese government policies help or hinder Bird's global competitiveness; how WTO concessions impact on Chinese handset manufacturers; and whether local agencies such as PCBP can continue to internationalize marketing communications services. It also depends on whether, and how, international consumer perceptions of products 'made in China' also shift. This depends on whether 'national champions' (such as Bird) can become internationally competitive in research and development. Until recently, Bird concentrated its research and development efforts on the fashionable

Table 4.1 Registers and contexts of global and local advertising appeals

	Register	
	Local	*Global*
Context	Somewhere	Anywhere
Values	Preserves Chinese cultural distinctiveness	Uses modernity and global cosmopolitanism to enhance social status ('face')
Symbolic meanings	Evokes traditional Chinese cultural values	Signals beauty, fashion, luxury and style
Product category	Everyday commodities, especially medicines, health supplements, food, non-alcoholic drinks	Luxury and status goods, jewellery, beauty products, luxury cars
Appeal	Rational emphasis on product attributes	Creative, emotional, entertaining
Models/ endorsements	Chinese models demonstrating filial loyalty, respect for the elderly, patriotic heroism	Non-Chinese models demonstrating Western values that are inconsistent with Chinese; otherwise Chinese models are acceptable

Source: derived from Zhou & Belk (2004).

appeal of handset casings. This was important in building market share by capturing the imagination of different domestic market segments. However, it is not a sufficiently knowledge-intense foundation from which to grow a global brand. China is considered the hub of the global cell phone handset industry, not only because it has the biggest market but also because international mobile phone manufacturers have considerable research and development capacity there. Chinese companies are not yet competitive in this area (Rose 2004) and building this capacity is important for global competitiveness. Responding to this challenge, in August 2003, Bird launched its 'smart' phone, the first to be fully engineered by a Chinese company. Content services and applications is another area that Bird has investigated.

Co-adaptation of advertising and value added cell phone services in China

As mobile markets mature, especially where competition on price has been intense, transnational handset manufacturers and carriers have turned to new content and applications services to maintain a competitive advantage. According to Chinese advertising industry scholar, Jing Wang, mobile music marketing was quickly selected as a development priority because '"musical taste" had become such an important demographic index for youth marketing in developed countries' (Wang 2005). Motorola was the first international brand to launch with this strategy in China in 2002, with its Moto campaign. This initiative aimed to establish the brand as the mobile entertainment choice for 'cool' Chinese youth. Motorola entered into joint ventures with MTV and Apple iTunes to enhance its music offerings. It also attempted to cement relationships with an elusive but highly desirable youth market with the development of its 'Emerging Artists' platform, which provided a forum for local 'new music talents who were seen as a bit edgy and somewhat removed from mainstream icons' (Wang 2005). The initiative was not a clear success for a variety of reasons; not least being the fact that there was an over-reliance on transnational assumptions about the global similarities of youth. Not enough attention was given to researching the particularities of Chinese middle class youth. Wang's own research found that 'age' was a far more reliable index than 'musical taste' for brand choices made by this group.

While transnational brands have greater know-how and wherewithal to develop new services, the Motorola experience exposed their vulnerability to competition from Chinese 'national champions' such as Bird and PCBP. The importance of local market knowledge cannot be overestimated, especially in a country as complex as China. In turn, local market knowledge can only become a competitive advantage where it can be translated into new content services and applications. The policy commitment to developing this capacity in advertising is most apparent. However, policy ambivalence for building an independent audiovisual production sector remains, largely because of anxiety about the unanticipated social consequences that may accompany this kind of development (Donald *et al.* 2002, 209). ICT applications and value added content service industries for mobile telecommunications have been treated more favourably. Nevertheless, this policy ambivalence may still impede a 'made in China' mobile content services strategy because these services rely heavily on re-purposing content that has already succeeded in other media markets. Constraints on local audiovisual industries may limit the supply of content for value added content services in the mobile space and compel value added service providers to source content from other, more developed international markets.

Another trigger for the interest in developing mobile data services has been the surprising and overwhelming popular success of Short Message Service (SMS), especially once debt-averse Chinese consumers obtained access to it on pre-paid services and all mobile carriers had achieved interconnection. As in other national markets, SMS paved the way for the development of a host of mobile data services, from ringtones to virtual pets, games, as a backchannel for broadcast media, and mobile marketing (Goggin and Spurgeon 2007). SMS also came to prominence in China when it was effectively used to disseminate information about the SARS outbreak in 2002. As network infrastructure is upgraded so too are the expectations for the future of mobile data services markets in China, especially those that attract premium rates above basic carriage charges.

Cell phone brand advertising in China informs consumers about the existence of a variety of handsets and value added services. It suggests ways in which offerings can enhance personal status and improve quality of life. Ultimately, however, cell phone brand advertising in China seeks to establish an affective connection with consumers that will influence brand choice when purchasing a handset. These strategies do not, on their own, explain the extraordinary adoption rates for mobile phones in China. Nor are they fully explained by the implementation of top-level plans to develop a consumer economy. We need to look at China's wider communication ecology in order to fully understand the popularity of the cell phone.

Until the commencement of the reform period in the late 1970s, fixed line telephone access was a luxury beyond the reach of the general Chinese population. Print and broadcast media were organized as state-controlled organs of mass-address. Access to non-Chinese media was generally restricted, because they were regarded as counter-revolutionary influences. In the past two decades, many of these restrictions have been eased, especially for the growing urban middle classes. Commercialization has expanded media choice. Chinese consumers are able to select from an expanding array of local and international niche media, and can avoid official Chinese media altogether, especially if they have the capacity to pay.

Cell phone services also massively expand the means and opportunities for mediated conversation. The accessibility that the technology affords to this form of interactivity is vitally important to comprehending its popularity.

As connections and user data suggest, mobile network connections are easier to obtain than internet connections, and are more affordable. Internet access may nevertheless be providing added impetus for cell phone adoption in China. By industry reckoning, half the world's internet users gain access via the mobile phone (Rosenzweig quoted in Elkin 2005). China is second only to the USA in terms of comparative numbers of internet users, even though only 8 per cent of people have internet access in China compared with 70 per cent of Americans. The number of cell phone connections relative to internet connections makes mobile internet services extremely attractive to carriers and content service providers, especially if they can be used to leverage premium charges. Advertisers are also very interested in the new platform, and global brands other than handset manufacturers are investing in advertiser-funded information and entertainment for mobile delivery to cell phones.

Adoption patterns for mobile and internet media and communications services, along with the anomalies and inequities of distribution, cannot be explained away as consequences of consumerism alone. They also reflect a popular desire for conversational social connection, for peer-to-peer communication that is unmediated by centralized media bureaucracies, irrespective of whether they are commercial or government-controlled.

When it comes to advertising in China, the explanatory power of theoretical frames of analysis that rely on the familiar dichotomies of Eastern and Western cultures, authoritarian and democratic political systems, command and consumer-centred economies, are also questionable. This is increasingly the case as new media markets develop and expand in China. As Chinese media studies theorists Stephanie Donald, Michael Keane and Yin Hong have observed:

> The impact of interactivity brought about by convergence of broadcasting, the Internet and telephony challenges assumptions about top-down flows of information. The shift from broadcasting to 'narrow-casting', the advent of broadband technologies and digital broadcasting, and the fact that Chinese people – like people elsewhere – can programme their own media rather than be captive audiences, disrupts the control metaphor.
>
> (Donald *et al*. 2002: 15)

The marketization of media and communications has accelerated the deployment of interactivity in China. However, it is highly unlikely that market forces will ensure equitable distribution of this capacity or that of other benefits of globalization and modernization. Indeed, rapid economic development appears to be exacerbating socio-economic disparities, especially between urban middle classes and rural poor. For example, while media services in metropolitan areas have grown exponentially, they have actually declined in rural areas, which are too poor to support advertising-funded media (Zhao 1998: 69).

Economic reform has had far-reaching social and political consequences, as the democracy movement, violently suppressed in 1989, indicates. But to suggest that this social movement is the consequence of marketization is to mythologize the relationship between markets and liberal democratic political systems in ways that are highly problematic. Martin Davidson describes this problem in slightly different terms. He argues that advertising is 'demotic rather than democratic' because it 'reflects diversity and not difference' (Davidson 1992: 202). The multi-dimensional complexities of social, cultural and political 'difference' are not to be confused with 'diversity', which is a more narrowly conceived means by which difference is managed. The Tiananmen Square demonstrations did not slow the marketization of the Chinese economy; it was precisely the kind of creative destruction of market forces that the Chinese government was relying on to stimulate the economic renewal of 'authoritarian liberalism', that is characteristic of, Chinese socialism. Donald, Keane and Hong use this term to describe a model of governmentality where,

> Chinese people have been allowed an increasing freedom to choose, to consume, and to be self-regulating, but where the authoritarian spectre of the disciplinary state remains as a fallback strategy of governance should civic freedom lead to anti-government uprisings.
>
> (Donald *et al.* 2002: 6)

Advertising is critically important to the creation and maintenance of markets and is shown here to play an important role in the development of new media circuits, especially in the wealthier coastal urban centres. However, it does not signify either the inevitable emergence of liberal democratic forms of government or enslavement in the service of global capital (Sinclair 1987). For the moment, advertising is as much a tool of central government control as ever, although its role in China's developing commercial culture is far more multifaceted and strategically important than it was in the three decades between 1949 and 1979. Advertising has prospered because central economic planners value it for the various ways in which it contributes to, and models, entrepreneurial, knowledge-based economic development. Similarly, consumption – the activity that advertising in its various guises ultimately seeks to influence – is regarded as an important engine of innovation in developing competitive, service-oriented market economies. Like markets, consumption can have multiple masters. For this reason, the ideological inflections assigned to consumption can be understood as symptoms of the wider social relations of economic and symbolic power within a given political system. The interests served by the rapid adoption and diffusion of new networked, conversational communications media, such as the cell phone, are even more varied.

Chapter 5

From conversation to registration

Regulating advertising and new media

Direct response advertising launched mobile content aggregator Jamba! on a rapid ascent to global infamy in 2004. Trading as Jamster in the English-speaking world, it quickly became synonymous with the 'Crazy Frog' animated character and ringtone.[1] Advertising for the ringtone and other Jamster mobile content appeared in a wide variety of mass and niche media, and reached saturation levels at various times. Jamster also advertised on the internet, in Web pop-ups and in promotional messages placed in chat environments. The strategy targeted young cell phone users in particular, and encouraged them to personalize their cell phones with Jamster mobile content, including ringtones and wallpapers. Other forms of Crazy Frog entertainment and merchandise were also heavily promoted and widely adopted into popular culture. In some countries this occurred with extraordinary speed and intensity. For example, in 2005 a commissioned dance single based on the Crazy Frog ringtone entered the UK music charts at No. 1 and held the top position for three weeks. The popularity of the Crazy Frog was reflected in extraordinary financial results for Jamster. It boosted Jamster's global sales from US$40 million in 2003 to US$500 million in 2005. However, by 2006 revenue was reported to have dropped back to about US$300 million. By this time, the global controversy about the Crazy Frog advertising strategy was beginning to catch up with Jamster.

The apparent offer of a free ringtone was a common feature of Crazy Frog ads. In fact, conditions applied, but these were usually specified in extremely fine print. It was not until the phone bill arrived, or credit on pre-paid plans mysteriously evaporated, that millions of teenagers and their parents began to understand that by responding to the offer they had also opted in to a 'club' to receive text messages (SMS) which were not free. They were premium rate services that attracted a charge in addition to the carriage cost. Charges varied from place to place, but were generally small enough to discourage individual consumers from investing the time necessary to take the matter any further than cancelling the club subscription, for example in taking formal action on the apparent deception, or recovering all the charges that had already been paid. One blog commentator described this strategy as 'a bait-and-switch scheme that turned looking at a ringtone into a "subscription" for costly spam messages' (Blankenhorn 2006). Jamster was not alone in promoting services in this way. However, the popular success of the Crazy Frog gave it the highest public profile of all mobile content aggregators.

The fact that switch-and-bait schemes could proliferate and prosper on such a large scale in new mobile media environments was due to the particular confluence of technological, commercial and public policy circumstances and interests of the time. The cell phone companies that provided billing and collection services in addition to carriage for third party service providers such as Jamster were often under intense pressure to achieve returns on their costly mobile spectrum investments in highly competitive markets. They also shared in the revenues that these schemes generated and were not necessarily empathetic, or particularly responsive, to consumer grievances about them. Indeed, it was not unknown for mobile content providers and carriers to respond to claims of misleading or deceptive practices in the premium rate services area, with the counter-claim that consumer discontent masked a more substantial underlying problem of consumer fraud. It was claimed that many consumers were perpetrating fraud against legitimate businesses by attempting to evade charges for services already rendered on terms they fully understood. Governments, who had reaped substantial windfalls from the creation of mobile spectrum markets, were also generally slow to perceive a need for consumer protection measures that addressed the problems of direct marketing and direct response advertising in, and for, new media services.[2] 'Light touch' regulatory agents were also reluctant to directly intervene. They were often charged with fostering economic growth through the development of new, technology-driven, global consumer markets and were also predisposed, if not required, to wait for mobile carriers, content and direct marketing industries to take the lead in shaping a regulatory response.

The case of Jamster illustrates the huge potential for mobile media in direct response advertising and direct marketing for a wide range of services, not just ringtones and wallpapers (Rao 2005). It also illustrates the downsides for consumers of these marketing communication techniques as they are adapted to new media environments, and points to an important dynamic in the co-adaptation of new media and advertising. On the one hand, direct response approaches to advertising are increasingly favoured by advertisers as a form of interactive advertising. On the other hand, response mechanisms are integral features of new media. They can function both as the channels for disseminating and repatriating information, and as the channels in which commercial transactions can occur. The channels of marketing communication and exchange are converging, and the Jamster case illustrates how the mobile data services environment was conditioned to support commerce from the outset (Goggin and Spurgeon 2007). This is an important point of contrast with the internet, which initially developed as a non-commercial research infrastructure and is only now being transitioned to a platform that is easily used and secured for commerce (Lessig 2006).

Direct response advertising is now widely recognized as a highly effective marketing communication technique, but in the mass media era it was largely marginalized as a marketing communication discipline for three main reasons. First, the costs of direct marketing media (mail and telephone) were generally prohibitive compared to mass media. Second, the high costs of direct media were often exacerbated by the dubious quality of available customer data. More often than not, data was sourced from

> list brokers, often acting as a cross between a quack doctor and a conjurer, taking a brief from a would-be direct mailer and, by some mysterious sleight-of-hand, producing, with a flourish, *exactly* the right list of people desperate to purchase the product or service the client was hoping to sell.
>
> (Berry 1998: 146)

Third, despite the successes of many reputable direct marketers who had built major businesses on long-term customer bases, the popular association of direct marketing with questionable high-pressure sales techniques and low production values generally dampened the interest of national brand advertisers.

Over the past two decades, however, the predisposition of major advertisers to direct marketing and direct response media has been turned about by rapidly developing markets for ICTs and services. The costs of direct advertising and marketing media have fallen dramatically, to the point that they are now highly competitive with mass and niche media costs. Falling data processing and storage costs have also facilitated the widespread adoption of service-based, customer-centred approaches to business. In addition to selling as many products to as many people as quickly as possible, it is increasingly cost effective to let consumers customize products and services to suit their specific needs and tastes. It is also possible to accumulate information about customers and to use this information to drive the ongoing development of goods and services. In this approach to enterprise, the customer base emerges as the primary asset of the firm (Peppers and Rogers 1997: 23), and developing the means for integrating all intelligence gathered from all sources of interaction with individual customers into searchable databases becomes a crucially important focus for investment (25). It is in this context that, as direct marketing expert Mike Berry observes, 'marketing information has become gold-dust and a whole industry has sprung up around the need to obtain it, improve it and use it with maximum cost-effectiveness as an essential marketing tool' (Berry 1998: 148).

New media enterprises are among the leading experts in consumer information because their businesses are built on the marketing value of the data repositories that they are amassing. As a result, the informational requirements and regulatory protections of the functional new media consumer citizen appear to be qualitatively different to those of the vulnerable mass media subject. The range of issues that are now swept up in the normative questions of informed consumer choice extend well beyond the effects of advertising texts, to how consumers come to be targeted by certain types of advertising in the first place. Claims to permission-based marketing and advertising are proliferating in many new media spaces. Yet the means for verifying these claims are far from uniform and, as the Jamster case illustrates, the remedies for failure remain underdeveloped. Many consumer citizens burnt by Jamster turned to the internet to share their experiences and advice on how to get redress, coordinating and publicizing more strategic responses; engaging directly with carriers; and prompting governments, regulators and the mass media to take action on their behalf.[3] Interesting and important in their own right, these efforts also speak to the weak negotiating position of the consumer citizen relative to the economic and political might of industry and government.

The case of Jamster reveals how the regulatory challenges of advertising and new media environments are made all the more complex by the global scale and scope of new media. Constraints upon the movement of information (including money) across borders are declining faster than local, state and national governments can summon the will to coordinate regulatory responses. More precisely, the will to regulate on an international scale is extremely one-sided in its practical effect. As Lessig (2006) argues, a range of comprehensive supra-national and national regulatory measures that protect the interests of copyright holders in new media contexts have been swiftly implemented. Schemes that might attempt to remediate imbalances in the social relations of new media from a more consumer citizen-centred perspective generally struggle to have any significant impact on the structure or norms of global markets.

Initial regulatory responses to premium rate services were often targeted at 'adult' content, as well as the inappropriate targeting of advertising for such content to young, impressionable people. The Jamster case made it clear that the inequity between the interests of mobile marketers and consumers was far more profound than instances of children accessing adult services via the phone, which content and advertising restrictions often addressed. Indeed, concerns about the effects and influence of media content on anonymous populations often obscure larger and more general questions, such as how end-user information stored in networks and the remote monitoring capabilities of networks are to be deployed.

This chapter draws on Lawrence Lessig's modes of regulation to look at how new media are being configured as direct marketing and advertising media.

Regulatory responses to the problem of unsolicited email (spam) reveal a high degree of ambivalence about the use of new media and communications for direct response advertising. First, though, the impact of ICTs on the informational orientation of advertising and new media is considered through the lens of Bordewijk and van Kaam's typology of interaction, discussed in Chapter 1. This helps to momentarily specify the object of regulatory concern as a particular type of interaction – registration. It is argued here that registration is an important technical means by which the norms of direct marketing are being quickly enabled as those of new media. It considers how the data-enhanced power of direct response advertising is being addressed in debates about the principles, scope and techniques of new media and communications regulation. Regulatory initiatives in these areas have been major tests of the influence of advertisers, direct marketers and new media in shaping the social relations of participation into the future. They are also occurring on a wide range of fronts, and draw advertising into broad debates about the information and privacy rights of consumer citizens.

Registration and the selling power of new media

Many current developments in electronic marketing communication rely on access to data that either resides in registration systems or is obtained by registration systems using remote monitoring applications in a variety of new media environments. As outlined in Chapter 1, interaction is understood in this book as a technological resource, with registration being one of four basic types of cybernetic interaction. Allocution, consultation and conversation are the others. Registration is essential to the efficient operation of many systems. In digital media and communications systems, registration is also the means by which remote monitoring and processing of consumer-generated information is automated. Programmatic control over the collection of information harvested by means of registration resides with the registration system, not the end-user. The billing and collection systems of utilities are probably among the oldest and most common examples of this kind of data capture and monitoring functionality. Telephone directories are another.

Registration is a type of surveillance that facilitates other types of interaction and exchange. It is the cornerstone of the 'world without secrets' (Hunter 2002) in which we now live, and is driven by the requirement of global commerce for an international personal identification and authentication system. It is the type of interaction upon which the direct marketing industry is built, and the foundation of integrated marketing communication (IMC) strategies. Previous chapters have canvassed the factors underlying strong consumer demand for conversational interaction as well as its implications for advertising and commercial media. Numerous examples have shown that where problems of scale and efficiency limit the practicality of actual conversation, registration technologies can provide a very effective substitute for conversation (for example, in search media and in the SMS voting feature of the Dove 'Campaign for Real Beauty'). Lawrence Lessig (2002) draws on his personal relationship with Amazon.com to illustrate the benefits of registration-as-conversation in advertising.

> I doubt any of your friends knows your tastes in music and books as well as Amazon knows mine. After a three-year relationship, dutifully remembered by Amazon's data-mining engine, Amazon can recommend to me things that I ought to buy. It advertises to me, but its advertisements – unlike 99 per cent of the ads I see in real space – actually speak to me. They actually say something that I want to hear. And because they speak to me, I listen.
>
> (2002: 133)

It matters little to consumers whether information comes in the form of an ad or an editorial if it is in some way useful. This point is not to be mistaken as an argument against the need for maintaining the distinction 'between advertising messages and the more disinterested entertainment and information functions of the media', which is also threatened with erasure (Dunn 2003: 133–4). Rather, in Lessig's experience of Amazon.com, registration helps to maintain a balance of interests between advertisers, the e-commerce medium and the consumer. It helps to 'conserve' consumer attention (Goldman 2006: 237). Lessig goes on to argue that the major social benefits of network economics are realized through the contributions that registration technologies make to reducing the costs of information in general, and advertising in particular. The costs of advertising historically favoured monopoly capital, because they presented a significant barrier to market entry when advertisers could only deal with costly mass commercial media. Registration helps to reduce these costs by improving the targeting of advertising and the tailoring of media so that advertisers can communicate with those who are most likely to be interested in their messages with increasing reliability and accuracy. Reductions in the cost of information are important in facilitating the market entry of new and small businesses. Thus, registration helps to lubricate the larger conversation of an efficient, competitive market.

However, not all new media users share Lessig's confidence that the beneficial uses of registration exceed the risks of more exploitative or sinister uses. As many unsuspecting respondents to ads for premium rate services have discovered, abuse of registration applications can have potentially highly damaging financial consequences. One of the early consumer problems with premium rate services is telephone 'bill shock', where a bill is substantially larger than anticipated. The causes of bill shock are varied, and can include unauthorized use of a premium rate service by a minor, with the subscriber, nonetheless, held liable. Subscribers can usually take measures to avoid bill shock, for example, by blocking premium rate numbers on their service. However, in many cases subscribers only take this step after an initial bill shock experience. In some cases, bills can be so high that they have caused serious financial hardship. Difficulties with premium rate services bills have also led to cancellation of telephone services and have impacted negatively on credit ratings (for example, TIO and BFSO 2005).

Spam is another particularly troublesome form of direct advertising, and is considered later in this chapter. Criminal uses of remote monitoring applications are also a substantial and growing source of concern. Tools such as 'keyloggers' repatriate key stroke data and have been implicated in various kinds of fraud including credit card fraud and identity theft (Hu and Dinev 2005), as have techniques such as 'phishing', which rely on consumer responses to apparently legitimate email requests for personal information (Lininger and Vines 2005).

In Chapter 1 it was noted that many early internet adopters strenuously resisted the commercial development of registration technologies designed to support development of new advertising-funded media. Castells (2002: 174) observes, however, that most internet users, like Lessig, seem generally willing to part with personal data but, unlike Lessig, the principle motivation is not necessarily to facilitate 'friction-free capitalism' (Gates 1996: 181). It is also exchanged for free access to internet content, communications services and server space, such as that which is provided by Google's Gmail, or content creation tools in social networks supported by sites such as MySpace, Yahoo websites such as Flickr, and Second Life.

New media use communications tools and social networks to make their services 'sticky'. Malcolm Gladwell (2002: 92) argues that 'stickiness' is the quality that successful advertising, like new media, needs to have in order to be effective in generating consumer responses. Without stickiness, the exit costs to consumers of new media can be very low to non-existent. For example, a consumer will not generally be worse off in economic or non-economic terms as a result of leaving one website to go to another. However, by using communication tools and the social network infrastructure of new media, end-users are encouraged to create their own incentives, as well as incentives for other visitors, to stay on a site for long periods of time. Thus, stickiness has a twofold benefit for new media. It can increase the exit costs to consumers of leaving a new media site and shifting to another provider (Humphreys 2005). It also supports the registration and accumulation of detailed longitudinal information about the habits of individual users, which in turn can be used to increase the stickiness of advertising content in the ways experienced by Lessig.

Registration and the co-adaptation of advertising and new media

As advertising and media continue to co-adapt, it is possible to discern not only the general diversification of interaction in the forms of consultation, conversation and allocution, but also an intensification of registration. For example, websites rely on a host of remote monitoring applications to track and develop unique profiles of visitors and to tailor the experience of subsequent visits. Subscription television services, which incorporate a return path in the configuration of their technical systems, also rely on registration and remote monitoring to develop 'addressable' and 'interactive' programming and advertising (for example, Gawlinski 2003; Cleland 2000; Kokernak 2000). As registration systems and remote monitoring applications become increasingly ubiquitous in other domains of everyday life, the capacity for marketers to correlate consumer data about new media and communication users with that obtained from other sources, including the supermarket scanner and the credit card, also increases (Phillips and Curry 2003; Gershman and Fano 2006). In addition to enhancing the accuracy and precision of targeting advertising, registration allows increasingly mobile and personalized media to function as a direct response mechanism for advertising. The advertising services of media are thus extended from exposing audiences to advertising messages (Gladwell 2002: 92) to eliciting direct responses.

Registration is used here to encompass a broad group of remote monitoring applications that have also been variously described as 'researchware' (Anon 2005), 'adware' and 'spyware' (DeMarco 2006; Shukla and Nah 2005). These applications are designed to repatriate information from network peripheries. These and many other major developments in registration technologies have been advertising-driven. However, this does not mean that remote monitoring applications are developed or used exclusively for marketing communication purposes. The term 'malware' has been coined to describe the malevolent or malicious uses of registration technologies (for example, Lininger and Vines 2005: 91; CTN 2006: 49–50) which do not appear to have any value whatsoever as market intelligence tools.

It is estimated that up to 90 per cent of computers connected to the internet are 'infected' with spyware (Awad and Fitzgerald 2005). But this does not mean that spyware is universally problematic. For example, a Web tracker downloaded to monitor the activities of an end-user without consent is spyware. However, if the same application is downloaded with the end-user's consent it is then more appropriately regarded as adware or, in some instances, researchware (Anon 2005). Indeed, an emerging consensus is now apparent in new media and advertising industries about the role of consumer consent in drawing these ethical, if not legal, distinctions.

Because context has such a significant impact on the operational definitions of remote monitoring applications, Awad and Fitzgerald (2005) choose instead to differentiate between them on the basis of whether or not they are conspicuous or inconspicuous to the end-user. Conspicuous applications include pop-up ads, or browser hijackers that change end-user computer settings. Inconspicuous applications can be installed and run without the end-user ever being any the wiser. These include cookies that monitor and facilitate movements within websites, or applications that track a user's movements across the Web.

There are also important distinctions to be made in the types of uses that are made of consumer data, as well as the data mining activities undertaken for marketing communication purposes (Goldman 2006). DeMarco (2006) draws a distinction between primary and secondary uses of consumer data gathered through registration, as well as direct and indirect uses. As Lessig's experience illustrates, registration applications can go unnoticed because e-commerce firms such as Amazon.com remain the primary users of the data they gather. Amazon's privacy notice emphatically assures users that it is not in the business of on-selling data to third parties for secondary purposes, but nevertheless reserves the right to vary this aspect of its terms of service without notice (Hunter 2002: 7). Amazon uses this information to personalize services. The data it gathers about individuals can be used anonymously and indirectly to improve services to market segments. This kind of data can be used to infer the demographic, psychographic and lifestyle characteristics that are extremely important to improving the effectiveness and efficiency of marketing communication (Spangler *et al.* 2006). These are examples of how inconspicuous, primary uses of registration can work successfully as an aid to conversational interaction and dialogic participation in markets.

The trade in data for secondary uses, such as aggregation, matching and profiling, has grown rapidly and offers new commercial media the potential to diversify revenue streams beyond advertising sales. Although conspicuous primary and secondary uses of information obtained by means of remote monitoring can be sources of great consumer annoyance, there is a tendency in marketing communication scholarship and industry literature to suggest that indirect secondary uses of data are tolerable because the consumer impact is largely benign (for example, Hu and Dinev 2005) while the benefits for business can be considerable. There are important exceptions, however. The growth of third party data specialists has proven to be particularly controversial for a number of reasons, including the extent to which they increase the risk of consumer exposure to unauthorized uses of de-anonymized data. Poor management practices of third party data specialists have been linked to serious crimes, such as identity theft (Sokolov 2005).

Castells (2002) suggests there is some level of end-user understanding that the price for personalized media is the surrender of a certain amount of personal information. Informed new media consumers know to consult the terms of service and privacy notices where these details are usually disclosed. Arguably, if these terms change, or do not satisfy an end-user's requirements, the end-user can go elsewhere for a similar type of service. Whether most users ever actually read and understand the terms of service is moot. Similarly, it is not always reasonable to assume that consumer exit costs from sticky new media environments are low.

The question of consent turns out to be vital to the task of categorizing and evaluating the legitimacy of registration and remote monitoring practices. Consumer awareness of privacy protection measures on the internet certainly appears to constrain internet usage (Zhang 2005), including the extent to which end-users will buy into the emerging social contract that requires the exchange of data for service. More contentious, however, are the types of mechanisms being used to obtain end-user consent. These can range from statements of the terms of service to software licences and End User Licence Agreements (EULAs). EULAs are a common form of agreement in multi-user online games. Software licence agreements are another important consent form. All of these mechanisms can be used to require an end-user to consent to remote monitoring as a condition of the service or licence (Warkentin *et al.* 2005; Stafford 2005, 101–4). Consent can cover the service provider for a range of primary and secondary marketing intelligence gathering and communication purposes. These activities can also serve a range of other purposes as diverse as including monitoring for copyright infringement and automating software updates.

Important questions about the extent to which the terms of many EULAs and licensing agreements are conscionable have yet to be thoroughly aired (Humphreys 2005). There are no apparent limits to the depth and breadth of remote monitoring to which an end-user should reasonably be expected to consent as a condition of service. Similarly, the uses made of data, are generally non-negotiable by end-users. Lessig describes this as a problem of the ways in which the 'presumptive controls' that individuals have over the data they reveal to others are set (Lessig 2006: 215). Sympathetic as he is to the productive role of registration in facilitating the operation of free markets, Lessig is critically aware of the extent to which the cumulative failures and successes of various modes of new media and marketing regulation inexorably result in presumptive control settings that favour the interests of commerce over broader social interests.

Spam regulation and the shaping of social participation

So far, this chapter has considered the importance of stickiness to the new commercial media business model, and the ways in which communication tools and end-user generated content contribute to this quality. Stickiness also facilitates consumer consent to remote monitoring and other forms of registration, which, in turn, can be used to improve the tailoring of services to very specific market segments and individuals, as well as the targeting of advertisements in personalized media services (Zarsky 2006). The discussion now turns to the technical development of registration functionality in what can be broadly described as the 'code' layer of media and communication systems, and a consideration of the ways in which this enhances the selling power of new media. The case of spam illustrates why code emerges as both an important object and as a mode of regulation in the new commercial media context.

Lessig (1999, 2002, 2006) draws on an engineering formulation of networks as a series of 'layers' to distinguish between the physical, code and content layers of a communications network. The physical layer includes the nodes and links that carry communication. The code layer is comprised of the protocols that specify how a network will work, as well as the applications that run on it. The content layer includes the communication that actually occurs on the network. Ownership, control and access (also called interconnection) to the physical layers of public communications networks emerged as major themes in communications law and policy debates in many parts of the world, especially in the 1980s and 1990s. Broad regulatory principles that recognized the importance of open and competitive networks to global markets were established during this period. These principles also shaped the conditions in which the internet exploded into the global mediascape. More precisely, Lessig argues, the particular constraints of four key modes of regulation – law, markets, network architecture (which he also calls code) and social norms – provided the conditions in which the phenomenal development of the internet could occur (Lessig 2006: 124). This mix saw the internet 'designed as an open system where network links between users were kept simple; intelligence and computing power were pushed to the ends of the network; and interfaces between users, content and networks were kept open and relatively transparent' (Winseck 2003: 181).

Lessig maintains that the most critical regulatory debates now concern questions of network architecture and code. Code, Lessig argues, is also the most significant mode of regulation in networks and network societies (Lessig 1999, 2006), because changes made at the level of code now have the most profound and far-reaching social consequences of any mode of regulation. For this reason, the code layer is the most important object of regulation. How network-based interactivity is governed, and how the rules of interaction are enacted through programming (code), underpins the terms of human agency and social participation in digital networks.

Different modes of regulation constrain some possibilities and permit others. The kinds of early internet spaces that were governed by norms and expressed in 'nettiquette' and Acceptable Use Policies, are now massively outnumbered by those that are governed by commercial contracts, which often take the form of terms of service agreements. Market forces now have a far more pervasive influence than social norms in shaping the terms of social participation in new media. Law can and does play an important role in new media regulation and, Lessig maintains, is most effective when used to require code-level compliance with normative expectations. This can be potently illustrated by considering the extreme problem of spam, a marketing communication technique that is having a significant influence on debates about how the internet is conditioned and regulated for commerce.

Direct marketing is built on the medium of direct mail (Berry 1998). The techniques that made direct mail a successful marketing technique have been translated to new media applications, most notably in email. Email reduces the costs of disseminating information almost to zero. The cost of acquiring large numbers of email addresses, either automatically harvested from the internet or purchased from third party vendors, is low. The cost of sending bulk email is even lower, especially when compared to the cost of physical mail. While the costs to advertisers have constrained the use of unsolicited addressed mail (junk mail), the volume of unsolicited email (spam) has grown exponentially since the mid-1990s, when commercial ISPs started providing public internet access. It is estimated that spam accounts for between 60 and 80 per cent of internet traffic, with the proportion varying from country to country (Lininger and Vines 2005: 25).

Spam doesn't 'clog' the internet as such, because text requires very little bandwidth, but it does clog mail servers (Gelman and McCandlish 1998). Filters and firewalls prevent most spam from reaching end-users. Without these technical, code-level interventions, the sheer volume of spam would threaten the viability of email as a communication platform as it would render email humanly impossible to manage (Wall 2004). Because email is now such an important business communication tool, spam threatens to compromise economic productivity significantly. In order to maintain viable email services, ISPs and third party email providers are compelled to commit substantial resources to managing spam. The US Federal Trade Commission considers spam to be 'one of the most intractable consumer protection problems' the regulator has ever faced (FTC 2005b: 3). Yet effective legal responses to spam have been curiously slow to emerge, especially when compared to the speed of responses to other apparently intractable problems, such as copyright protection in networked digital media environments (Lessig 2006: 337).

There are many different sources of spam. Bulk unsolicited commercial email was the predominant early form of spam. These days the problem of spam is significantly exacerbated by malware, such as virally-disseminated, self-executing spam generators, or by email fraudsters phishing for personal information. Nevertheless, email is still regarded as an extremely valuable direct marketing tool (for example, Mullin 2002). A relatively small number of people appear to be responsible for most phishing scams and large bulk commercial e-mailings (Spamhaus Project 2007). Code-based spam controls such as filters, firewalls and 'baffle bots' (Bruno 2003) aim to deal with all sources of spam. Legal controls also address both commercial and nuisance forms and clarify the circumstances in which bulk unsolicited commercial email is permissible. They have the effect of legalizing certain kinds of spam (Ford 2005). This reflects the early and generally consistent success that direct marketers, particularly in the USA, have had in arguing the legitimacy of unsolicited bulk email (for example, Lynch 1997).

There have been important jurisdictional variations in the speed and scope of international legislative responses to the problem of spam. The UK *Privacy and Electronic Communications Act* came into force in late 2003, pursuant to the European Union's Privacy and Electronic Communication Directive. Australian anti-spam legislation was introduced in 2003. In the USA, a number of states were early movers on spam, but these laws were eventually largely pre-empted by the federal *Controlling the Assault of Non-Solicited Pornography and Marketing Act* (CAN SPAM), which took effect in January 2004. Anti-spam laws around the world have many common features. They generally criminalize spamming and require bulk emails to be identified as such. Where bulk unsolicited email is generated for legitimate commercial communication purposes, it must include a functional means for an end-user to request that that they be removed from a marketer's email distribution list, and such requests must be complied with. The commercial use of email address harvesting software is generally prohibited. This activity is recognized internationally as a major factor contributing to the prevalence of spam, both commercial and malevolent (FTC 2005a). In other words, spam laws seek to constrain the presumption of control over end-user data, particularly email addresses, in very specific ways. Anti-spam laws generally make provision for international cooperation among national regulators for the purpose of eliminating criminal uses of email (FTC 2005b). They are also usually sufficiently expansive to apply to electronic unsolicited bulk commercial communications in a range of contexts, for example mobile platforms and developing internet applications such as Voice over Internet Protocol (VoIP) (FTC 2005b).

However, there are important differences between national jurisdictions. In the USA and Australia, for example, certain classes of bulk email creators, such as political parties, charities and educational institutions, are exempt from anti-spam laws. This, arguably, compromises the effectiveness of anti-spam measures (Arora 2006). The most significant difference arises in the detail of the presumption of control over end-user information. In the USA, the presumption is set in favour of bulk emailers. The federal anti-spam law permits a bulk emailer to presume that a recipient wants unsolicited email until such time as the recipient requests to 'opt-out' from receiving email from a specified source. In the UK, Europe and Australia, bulk email can only be legally sent to those who have consented, or 'opted-in', to receive it in the first place (and have not subsequently elected to 'opt-out').

The federal US 'opt-out' approach is widely regarded as the lower threshold. Some commentators have argued that because US-based spammers find it easier to continue to operate, for all practical purposes the US 'opt-out' approach has become the global standard for presumptive control over email addresses (Dettmer 2003). Certainly it appears that the most prevalent and problematic sources of spam originate in the USA (Spamhaus Project 2007). Even though the UK and Australian approaches appear to be tougher, they are still seriously flawed. Requirements for clarity about consumer consent to 'opt-in' are open to broad interpretation by marketers. This was one of the many problems of the Jamster mobile content 'clubs'. It was not always clear to consumers that in responding to the ringtone offer they were also 'opting-in' to receive other messages from Jamster. That consumers were paying to receive apparently unsolicited messages added injury to insult.

Despite initial implementation problems, the number of successful civil and criminal prosecutions of spammers is increasing (for example, Anon 2006c; Chabrow 2005; Wendland 2003). There is general agreement that as long as technical, code-based solutions can keep up with the innovations in spam techniques, they are generally more effective than legal measures (Ahmed and Oppenheim 2006; Bruno 2003; FTC 2005a; Swartz 2004; Berghel 2006). However, whether evolving technical or existing legal solutions are staunching the flow of spam in the first place is debatable (Dickinson 2004; Gross 2005).

The use of registration to authenticate email is one of a number of options being seriously considered as a way to effectively regulate spam. One option that has attracted considerable attention is the idea of a fee or tax on email (Cappo 2003: 183). A tax or fee would provide a strong cost-based disincentive for spamming. Arguably, it would also build public confidence in email and, by encouraging the ongoing adoption of email, 'would replenish the commons on which the spammers themselves subsist' (Hirsch 2006: 248). However, this development pre-supposes that the identity of email originators will always be made discoverable by fee or by tax collectors. In practical terms, the registration and authentication systems that such a measure would require might be all that is needed to effectively combat spam without resorting to the imposition of a tax or fee on email. These would render email originating from unauthenticated sources (as a lot of spam does) instantly undeliverable.

The idea of rebalancing the economics of email so that senders, rather than receivers, bear the costs of email, particularly spam, is being actively explored by

ISPs and email service providers. In 2006, Yahoo! and America Online (AOL) announced plans to introduce a fee for bulk email on the grounds that it would be an effective initiative in the war against spam (Hanseel 2006). The measure would authenticate unsolicited commercial communication and clearly differentiate it from other non-commercial forms of spam, such as phishing emails. The practical effect of this initiative was seen to be giving preferential treatment to bulk e-mailers who are willing and able to pay a fee to bypass AOL spam filters (Goldsborough 2006). This has echoes of the mass media model, where media sell advertisers access to largely undifferentiated audiences.

Systematic development of email authentication is a controversial development, because it forecloses on the possibility of anonymous interaction and participation on the internet. Anonymous interaction was one of the highly prized normative values of early internet cultures for which its early designers explicitly provided (Bellovin 2004; Cerf 2005). Yet network-based commerce has much to gain from a more systematic approach to the development of authentication technologies for the internet. Numerous initiatives are in progress, including one being championed by Microsoft that seeks to add an 'Identity Layer' to the internet (Lessig 2006, 50ff.). Developed along open source principles, an Identity Layer could theoretically allow consumers to exercise far more precise control over the release of their own authentication data than they are presently afforded. It could make the internet a more trustworthy environment for a range of uses, not just commercial transactions. For example, it could be used to ensure that minors do not get access to restricted content, and to manage spam.

Lessig regards the development of Internet Protocols for managing an Identity Layer as a potentially 'brilliant solution' (Lessig 2006: 51) to balancing the competing interests of commerce and consumercitizens on a range of fronts. Lessig qualifies this support with the caveat that this approach can only work if the default setting for presumptive control over end-user data favours the end-user and not registration systems. In other words, the governing code for such a layer needs to be 'privacy enhancing' for individuals (Lessig 2006: 226), and not simply a means for facilitating commercial and bureaucratic interests in the end-user information generated by network usage. In effect, Lessig is arguing that Privacy Enhancing Technologies (PETs) have the potential to provide the systemic correction that is necessary to achieve a self-regulating balance of the various interests in registration technologies.

The systematic incorporation of authentication into the code layers of the internet can be approached as either a glass half-emptied or a glass half-filled by privacy rights. On the one hand, it represents a fundamental re-purposing of the internet to facilitate commerce; on the other hand, it amounts to little more than a consolidation of all the incremental and cumulative changes to the internet that have been achieved through the use of registration technologies to date, including those briefly outlined in this chapter. In either approach, authentication is no less problematic or in need of systematic regulatory attention than other forms of registration considered here: remote monitoring and marketing databases. The modes of regulation best suited to these challenges are very much in contention. Initiatives in authentication are important illustrations of the privatization of cyberlaw, where the terms of social participation coded into the network society are profoundly shaped by the private domains of large Internet Service Providers. Dwayne Winseck (2003) argues that industry-based agreements about the default settings for PETs are highly technocratic and individualistic responses to the problems of privacy that surveillance raises. They introduce 'another dimension of social hierarchy into cyberspace', based on technocratic knowledge and expertise. This 'leaves the surveillance imperatives being designed into information infrastructure unscathed' (188). He maintains, 'it is far more important to address the absence of adequate legal protections for personal information' (188). Winseck points to the critical concern that direct marketing industry norms, expressed in codes of industry conduct, increasingly prevail as the norms for regulating registration in the code layers of networks and in the laws governing the terms of social participation in them.

New media as direct response media

Email, the Web and mobile phones are the new media of direct response advertising and direct selling. There is nothing particularly new about the concepts or practices of direct response advertising or marketing. Although historically these marketing communication strategies have deployed 'above-the-line' media, such as television and magazines, they were most strongly associated with 'below-the-line' media, such as mail (addressed and unaddressed) and telemarketing. From a marketing perspective, the data generated from the in-built registration systems of post and telecommunication networks was the important point of difference between mass and direct response media. Enhanced and expanded with the 'new logistics' (Mattelart 2002: 24) of ICTs and searchable databases, the new media not only offer new levels of accountability but also potentially offer very detailed and valuable insights on markets. The example of spam illustrates the ways in which technological change has contributed to a significant shift in the economics of direct marketing and advertising methods. Crucially, as the Jamster example illustrates, new media are also support exchange, not only for conversational interaction but also for participation in markets, for the buying, selling and delivering of informational goods and services.

The direct mail industry was significantly aided by the development of zip and postal codes to define, classify and target market segments on the basis of their geodemographic characteristics (Phillips and Curry 2003). Telemarketing is as old as the telephone itself, but really came into its own with the aid of toll-free numbers (Berry 1998: 9) and technological improvements, which proliferated as the monopoly controls over the public switched telephone network were removed. Automatic dialling and voice-activated response systems have seen the incidence of telemarketing rise to nuisance levels, provoking regulatory responses in many places, with varying degrees of success (Anon 2003). Cable television spawned the 'infomercial' (Cappo 2003: 174) and the internet gave rise to unsolicited e-mail or spam. Where direct mail and the infomercial were generally beneficial to their post and cable hosts, spam threatens to destroy email on the internet. It could have similarly dire consequences for cell phones. In the main, direct marketers are trying to apply the lessons of the internet to mobile technologies (Sangster interview 2005). While they are extremely keen to gain access to this intimate personal space, there is also a shared understanding that, unless access is based on a clear invitation, direct marketers could very probably kill the mobile golden goose. This understanding is reflected in industry codes of conduct and in legislative restrictions on the use of unsolicited commercial messages in mobile, as well as fixed network, environments. However, the effectiveness of industry self-regulatory approaches to maintaining a wider public interest in accessible, affordable and trustworthy new media and communications services is, at times, questionable.

There is a strong tendency to address concerns about surveillance in general, and registration technologies and applications in particular, in terms of their implications for individual privacy. However, this approach can blind us to the broader social consequences of compromising individual privacy. This is one of the key themes of a growing body of scholarship which argues that privacy protections alone are not adequate responses to the social consequences of registration. Oscar Gandy, one of the early critical scholars to develop this line of argument in his 1993 book *The Panoptic Sort*, highlighted the discriminatory effects of database marketing, whereby data about transactions were collected for the purpose of targeting individuals for further advertising while avoiding those of little or no value to marketers. 'Social sorting', as David Lyon so elegantly describes it, relies on the searchable database to guide the operation of 'the invisible doors that permit access to or exclude from participation in a multitude of events, experiences and processes . . . The gates and barriers that contain, channel and sort populations and persons have become virtual' (2003: 13).

David Phillips and Michael Curry (2003) argue that there is much more at stake here than problems of intrusion into personal space. Exposure to unwanted bureaucratic market management, which increases the ease of social discrimination based on location, race, gender and income, is something that also deserves policy attention. Just as important is the matter of where and how the line is drawn between privacy issues that are to be regulated at the level of the individual and those that are to be legislated for by taking into account a broader view of the social consequences of social sorting. Where registration data is presently held to be a matter of individual preference, responsibility for ensuring adequate minimum levels of privacy protection actually defaults to the media and marketers. Informed individuals can adopt, adapt and personalize technical solutions to meet their particular needs, but only to the point that consent mechanisms permit. Beyond that, service providers reserve a contractual right to deny access. These are the limits of a privatized cyberlaw. The Jamster case illustrates some of the social dilemmas of industry-based regulation of registration including how, and whether, industry-determined default settings on the collection and use of registration data might realistically be relied on to ensure that children and young adults are not unfairly directly targeted.

Direct marketers have adapted rapidly to new media and are driving the development of searchable databases and social surveillance. The efficiency and effectiveness dividends of these developments to marketers have seen their methods and strategies move quickly from the margins to the mainstream of marketing, with the database forming the core focus of the marketing effort. In recent decades many services sectors have integrated direct marketing into their marketing communication and business strategies, including financial and communications services (Berry 1998). The intensification of this trend corresponds with the mass adoption of new media. Matthew McAllister (1996: 15) argues that the movement to integration can be understood as a response to the loss of control many advertisers believed they had previously exercised over mass media audiences and environments. It is an attempt to reassert control, this time leveraging the registration rather than the transmission capabilities of digital media and communications.

Chapter 6

The future of advertising-funded media

The global media and entertainment conglomerate News Corporation acquired a controlling interest in mobile content aggregator, Jamster, in 2006 for $US188 million. Made infamous and highly profitable by its signature 'Crazy Frog' ringtone, the deal anticipated the vertical integration of Jamster's global mobile content production, marketing, sales and distribution capabilities with News Corporation's media and entertainment properties. News Corporation's President and CEO Peter Chernin described the merger as 'an important step in News Corp.'s strategy of becoming the world's leading digital media company' (News Corporation 2006). It is worth contemplating the origins and implications of News Corporation's new media strategy because it indicates a major development trajectory for the advertising-funded media business model. This sees commercial media exploring and developing their potential as marketing agents, not just as advertising media.

Jamster substantially strengthened the position of News Corporation at the leading edge of mobile premium rate services development. The premium rate business model is, at one level, a variation of the user-pays business model often associated with multichannel television. In industry vernacular, it is also described as a micropayments system, but one that emanates from telecommunications rather than the internet. For the moment, premium rates services are the principle means by which cell phone-based media and entertainment applications, offered in proprietary 'walled' content gardens, are commercialized. There is significant potential for free, advertiser-funded content and for peer-to-peer networks of consumer-generated premium rate content, but these have not been high developmental priorities to date. Importantly, technological convergence means this business model can, potentially, be integrated across all electronic media. It is already widely embedded in television formats and, as such, is an important ancillary revenue stream for the producers and broadcasters of programmes such as *Idol*, *Big Brother* and many others (Spurgeon and Goggin 2007; Nightingale and Dwyer 2006). The significance of the premium rate business model is its capacity to switch the electronic media channel to a direct response, transaction and service delivery channel. It enables electronic advertising media to change from being virtual display windows of goods and services to being channels for the direct sale and distribution of electronic information and entertainment content and services. It also paves the way for mobile commerce (m-commerce) developments.

For media, the premium rate business model diversifies revenue streams by generating a transaction-based commission directly from consumers. This commission is repatriated along the premium rate service value chain. Media are an important part of this value chain, as are telephone companies and new mobile marketing and content intermediaries such as Jamster. By taking a direct interest in this value chain News Corporation is, in effect, buffering its exposure to the risks of heavy reliance on advertising revenue. It also opens up opportunities to develop new, customized and personalized cross-platform pay and subscription services. More significantly, it illustrates how the boundaries between advertising clients, agencies and media, once carefully maintained by these stakeholders, are blurring (Sinclair 2006: 120). In the case of News Corporation, its new media investments suggest an intensification of its broader positioning as an integrating entertainment, media and marketing enterprise.

There are at least four other main new media business models in addition to premium rate services, of which advertising persists as the most substantial income source for market-based media enterprises in the digital era. 'Old' media businesses need to work out how to deploy new communication services in order to maintain and develop markets, and to leverage the productivity of new media consumers. New media expand the range of services that commercial media need to offer to consumers in order to remain viable. The mix of 'content' and 'contact' services (Middleton 2002) becomes an important point of differentiation between media. It also has important consequences for the types of content and communication services that will find favour with consumer markets and advertisers. Nevertheless, the acquisition, production and distribution of media content will continue to be central to many media businesses. Other business models, which might help to fund this expanded array of offerings, include subscription services, sales and commissions from one-off purchases of content or service access, and sales of ancillary goods and services such as merchandise (Harris 2007). The business imperative to spread risks means that developing revenues from all these sources is important to most media enterprises, but advertising continues to be crucial simply because it accounts for the largest proportion of revenues for most commercial media businesses.

Adapting services to meet the needs and interests of advertisers in the digital environment is a major challenge now confronting commercial media. This is not limited to the task of attracting, maintaining, mobilizing and marketing the affective labour of media consumers. It entails the diversification and integration of the range of techniques for facilitating advertiser–consumer interaction. Out of the recent history of global consolidation of advertising, media and entertainment industries have come new opportunities and pressures to disintermediate the advertising value chain. New, as well as reconfiguring commercial media are appropriating some roles that were previously fulfilled by agencies. The momentum unleashed by digitization, global consolidation and convergence to reorganise national and international advertising and marketing communications service industries, as well as media and entertainment industries, is not slackening.

Digitization has been a key technological condition of both convergence and globalization. Convergence continues to be an important driver of globalization, and is also facilitated by it. Convergence is apparent at three key levels: at the functional level of technology, in products and services, and in the industries that use and produce digital technologies, products and services (Flew 2002: 17–21). The pace of technological and service convergence is apparent in the cycles of rapid consumer market development, growth and maturation for multi-purpose communication devices. Cell phones, for example, now routinely double as personal data assistants, as cameras that capture still as well as moving images, and as navigation tools. They can be used to access internet services, or to receive mobile television, in addition to voice, text and other telephone-based data services.

Global consolidation of assets, services and industries, was a feature of international capital in the1980s and was, in part, a response to the risks associated with the scramble into new markets, including former Soviet bloc countries. Like other service industries, advertising agency networks kept pace with the expansive ambitions of their globalizing clients in this period. By the early 1990s most major national and international agency networks were owned and managed by handful of global 'megagroups' (Sinclair 2006: 113). At the start of the new millennium, more than half of the world's advertising and marketing expenditures passed through the accounts of four of these groups – the Omnicom Group, Publicis, the Interpublic Group of companies and the WPP Group (Cappo 2003: 11). Inherent to the global consolidation of advertising were the twin tendencies of industry convergence: horizontal integration and specialization. Global consolidation affected all marketing communication disciplines, from public relations to direct marketing, and facilitated the development of integrated and 'through the line' approaches to marketing communication. Jo Cappo estimates that disciplines other than traditional advertising now account for up to half the turnover of the major holding companies (Cappo 2003: 46). Media buying and creative services were disaggregated from the full service agency structure, partially in response to client expectations of greater transparency in agency cost accounting practices.

By the 1990s, new technologies and a new, neoliberal regulatory mood precipitated a proliferation of media and entertainment choices in the major European and North American markets. Media choices were also expanding in other rapidly developing consumer markets in many parts of Asia. These developments accelerated the trend to global consolidation in media, entertainment and communications industries. Five global media and entertainment giants emerged in this period of expansion – Time Warner, Disney, Bertelsmann, Viacom and News Corporation (Herman and McChesney 1997: 70ff.). The fragmentation of media 'tended to diminish the effectiveness of advertising' but also opened up new opportunities for 'a more far-reaching subsumption of the productivity of consumers' (Arvidsson 2006: 75) into the integrated brand management strategies of advertisers, including those of the media and entertainment conglomerates themselves. Global consolidation in media and entertainment industries aimed, in part, to achieve new economies of scale for existing products and services, and economies of scope for the development and promotion of new ones.

The integrated marketing communication opportunities that were created in the global consolidation of media and entertainment industries favoured a particular kind of cultural commodity, which P. David Marshall describes as 'intertextual' (Marshall 2004). Examples of intertextual commodities include *Harry Potter*, *Lord of the Rings*, *Lara Croft* and *Hilary Duff*. These function as 'content brands', according to Adam Arvidsson, because 'they travel between and provide a context for the consumption of a number of goods or media products' (Arvidsson 2006: 75). The branding strategies for these commodities rely on the communicative and social productivity of consumers to circulate and develop brand identity and value, and to support an array of brand extensions and merchandise. Investments in social networks such as MySpace expand the market potential for intertextual commodities. Not only does MySpace provide News Corporation with a platform for trend-spotting and hit-making, but it also facilitates consumer involvement in the development and management of new content brands, as discussed in further detail shortly.

The growth of markets for intertextual commodities only indicates the partial success of the globalization strategy for media and entertainment industries. Content is re-purposed very efficiently and effectively across commonly owned and operated platforms and networks. The integration of content and content systems, which predicated the growth of intertextual commodities, has generally been very successful. However, globally consolidated media still struggle to achieve the same level of integration for advertisers (Cappo 2003). The contrast with new search media is striking. Google and Yahoo!, for example, have enjoyed far greater success in developing integrated solutions for advertisers than media and entertainment conglomerates.

Search media quickly established that the internet could work as an advertising medium, not just as a platform for e-commerce. This breakthrough came from a number of major innovations associated with the development of search media, particularly in media buying. Media sales based on the cost per click and auction-based pricing of media inventory have proven to be extremely successful. These innovations have been highly advantageous to many advertisers, small and large, despite the risks of manipulation indicated by problems such as click-fraud. They are significant for at least three reasons. First, in systematizing performance and transaction-based charging for media they introduce new currencies to the advertising trade in new media consumers. Second, they increase the accuracy of estimating the return on advertising investment in ways that are potentially more precise than the pricing measures and mechanisms of mass and niche media. Third, integration across a vast network of properties has the effect of establishing large media buying markets. The media buying markets supported by Google, for example, are not limited to selling commonly owned media that use the same delivery platforms, as is more usually the outcome of the integrated advertising sales solutions so far developed by global media and entertainment conglomerates. Although largely confined to the internet at present, transaction and auction-based pricing of media has great potential for general application across all media platforms, including print media and broadcast radio and television. Furthermore, advertisers and online media, especially those operating in the global niches of the new economy, are driving movement along this trajectory of change.

The mounting pressures on the current advertising-funded business models of incumbent mass and niche media are far more complex than data about the rapid movement of revenues into online advertising at first suggest. Adaptation strategies need to address simultaneously the rapidly changing media usage patterns of advertisers, as well as consumers, by engaging with the underlying, disparate and sometimes competing interests they reflect.

Throughout this book it has been argued that the changes in the media and communication choices of consumers can be broadly characterized as a shift from 'mass media' to 'mass conversation'. Worldwide, levels of consumer demand for media and communication services, such as those enabled by the internet and cell phones, have been extraordinary and unprecedented (Sciadas 2005: 8–11; World Bank 2006: 3–5). Digital technologies and global telecommunications markets appear to have achieved, in a few short decades, improvements in the accessibility and affordability of conversational media that eluded a century of centrally planned progress in analogue communications. The rapid adoption and diffusion of these new media of mass conversation is highly disruptive for mass media. One important consequence is that transmission is denaturalized as the commonsense approach to organizing media and communications infrastructure and service development. Just as the privileged status of advertising among marketing communication disciplines was altered in the processes of globalization, so too is the radical monopoly of media transmission being undone. Transmission remains an important resource, but it needs to be understood as just one of many possible architectures of interaction.

Consumer demand for conversational interaction and social engagement has significant consequences for the advertising revenues of media based on other types of interaction. As discussed in Chapter 1, print media are principally based on consultation, and broadcast media principally rely on transmission. Networked digital media such as cell phones and the internet open up at least three new technical possibilities for electronically mediated interaction on a mass scale, and their equivalent opportunities for social participation. Two of these are conversation, which is based on the possibility of reciprocal exchange, and intercreativity, which allows for the ability of end-users to be directly involved in media as producers, not just as users or consumers. Both were seriously constrained by the technologies, politics, economics and social organization of mass media for most of the twentieth century. Registration – or remote monitoring of interaction – is another type of interaction that has been made more affordable and ubiquitous by developments in ICTs. It provides the means by which digital media platforms can be personalized, used as consumer profiling technologies and made to function as channels for commerce.

Conversation is the core type of interaction supported by telecommunications networks. Initially developed as a business tool, the telephone was adopted in the second part of the twentieth century as an indicator of economic inclusion and social participation in modern society (World Bank 2006: 2). Although it was widely regarded as a necessity, the costs and logistics of fixed telephone infrastructure meant that distribution patterns for telephone services corresponded with those of wealth and privilege. Once markets for digital wireless services started to be created in the 1990s, these barriers were dramatically lowered, and mass markets in conversational media took off around the world. While the specifics of market and service development vary from place to place, the strength of consumer demand for cell phones reflects an unmistakable desire for conversational interaction. Similarly, from the time that modems could be used to access the internet over telephone networks, consumer markets for this new platform, and the multipatterned array of possibilities for end-user controlled interaction it supports, have also boomed. By no means, however, is everyone, everywhere, connected for conversation. The 'digital divide' is real, however it might be defined – in terms of economic, physical, or knowledge-based limits on access to communication technologies. It traces the historical and geopolitical inequities at the core of the global economy. Conversely, consumer demand for access to conversational media points to a deep and widely held human desire for social engagement, and for a 'voice' that can be heard (Tacchi 2005: 25).

The strength of this human desire for conversation is reflected in the emerging social contract between new commercial media and their users. Like old media, new commercial media make their money from packaging media consumers for sale to advertisers. The important difference is that communication and content creation tools are now offered alongside, and in place of, the 'free lunch' of mass media content. New media consumers schedule, make and distribute their own media services, and simply bypass media that cannot or do not support conversational interaction. Remaining competitive by acquiring conversational capabilities increases top line costs for old media. However, it also extends to them the advantages that accrue to new media from registration. In order to participate in the smorgasbord of mass conversation media consumers must register for it, and in the process consent to service provider monitoring and control of the data that their participation generates. This data has immense value to media proprietors who want to customise the media–consumer relationship, and to advertisers who want highly targeted access to their markets. There are in existence in many parts of the world statutory and regulatory limits that can constrain the terms of this bargain, and the uses that can be made of end-user information. Third party access to this data nonetheless looms as a major issue for policy and regulation. Many problems of registration can be partially ameliorated by the adoption of consumer-centred presumptions of control over information in the development of authentication technologies for e-commerce. The continuing development of clearly articulated, enforceable and globally coordinated consumer protection regimes nevertheless remains vital to building trust in new, networked media.

There are also important factors of generational change associated with the rise of conversational media. When given the choice, young people mostly make the 'DIY' choice (Hartley 1999). The aging demographics for newspaper readerships and television audiences suggest that the media habits of older generations are not as easily altered. The fact that the early adopters of conversational media also happen to count among the most coveted demographics for advertisers (young, educated and with high disposable incomes) was an important incentive to commercialize digital media platforms in the first place (Cappo 2003: 200). The movement of these highly desirable demographics away from mass media similarly provides a powerful motivation for mass and niche media to adapt. Oscar Gandy (1993) argues that this pattern of media development has the effect of increasing choice for a very narrow range of consumers but reduces choices for others. Influential claims have been made about the extent to which the 'long tail' effects of new media economics counter these tendencies of niche marketing (Anderson 2004). This logic asserts that the physically unbounded capacity of e-commerce means that all interests can be profitably addressed in ways that contribute to the health of media diversity. These claims remain to be critically evaluated and tested.

John Pavlik (1998) identifies four main adaptation strategies used by globalizing and digitizing media conglomerates. Increased specialization allows a media organization to concentrate efforts on targeting its identified core audience. Reformatting existing content in new formats is one way to extend the shelf life of content libraries and to develop new markets for this content. Developing new applications and tools for new platforms is another adaptation strategy. Acquisitions and mergers are another relatively quick way to build a presence on new distribution platforms and to develop new markets. All of these strategies are apparent in the recent and more distant history of News Corporation. Print and electronic media, along with Hollywood entertainment, are News Corporation's bread and butter, but News Corporation also has an interesting historical relationship to new media. It has often occupied the position of the new entrant in a media market, and has an extraordinary track record of taking a long-term view in the process of adapting the advertising-funded business model to new, but often high-risk, media platforms and market opportunities. In Australia, it established the third commercial television network; in the USA, the fourth; and in Asia and the UK it was an early entrant into satellite distribution platforms.

When News Corporation acquired the social networking site MySpace in 2005 for $US580 million there was a great deal of speculation about whether an 'old' media corporation could do anything other than destroy it. In fact, the MySpace network continued to grow exponentially, and the shrewd business judgement of Murdoch and his digital media executives was affirmed soon after when a $US900 million deal was struck with Google. This gave the search juggernaut exclusive rights to sell advertising on Fox Interactive Media properties, including MySpace, for three years. In effect, the expertise to integrate advertising services across these new media properties was bought in, complementing the 'in-house' strength in developing and marketing intertextual content brands.

Established in 2003 and initially promoted as a site used by unsigned bands to build and maintain direct, fan-based markets, MySpace quickly grew to become a major online advertising site in its own right. At the time that the News Corporation purchase was announced, new users were reported to be joining MySpace at a rate of 3.5 million each month, and the site was hosting more than 10 per cent of all Web ads (Hove 2005). The deal with News Corporation was controversial, not least because it roughly coincided with legal action against the MySpace parent company, Intermix, for alleged misleading and deceptive advertising practices. The New York State Attorney-General had reportedly identified Intermix as the most 'egregious purveyor of spyware' (Ante *et al.* 2005). The timing of the sale led to claims and counterclaims that News Corporation had bought MySpace for a fire sale price (Greenspan 2006). The controversy also raised questions about the motivations behind the establishment of MySpace, as primarily a social network or a get-rich-quick direct marketing platform (Lapinski 2006).

The commercial value of social networks such as MySpace is not only as channels for communicating advertising messages. They can also be used as market research platforms in their own right. Indeed, many accounts of the early history of MySpace suggest that it was established as a new kind of advertising medium: one where consumers were conceived as advertisers, and where advertisers would be invited into the quasi-private worlds of young consumers. Even though the search advertising deal with Google made a windfall return for News Corporation, the real value of MySpace is the way in which it positions News Corporation as the 'host of the cultural conversation' (Reiss 2006). MySpace opens up unprecedented opportunities for News Corporation to capture market intelligence that will be highly valuable for cross-platform marketing of News Corporation content brands, as well as those of other advertisers. It significantly enhances News Corporation's specialist knowledge in media targeted to youth demographics. In future, News Corporation could more closely resemble a specialist youth marketing company than a media and content company (Reiss 2006).

Underpinning anxieties about News Corporation's acquisition of MySpace were concerns that it would stifle the vibrant social network site and cause its nascent innovation culture to stagnate. The concern for MySpace participants was over the burden of exit costs they might face if changed terms and conditions of involvement created disincentives and obstacles to participation. The business concern was whether the marketing potential of the site would be fully realized. In innovation cultures this potential is not limited to the intertextual commodity. It extends to the production of what P. David Marshall describes as 'indiscrete' cultural commodities (Marshall 2004). The exemplar of this class of commodities is computer games. These are co-created in the process of being played, rather than consumed (Kline *et al.* 2003; Herz 2005). They rely far more directly and extensively than intertextual commodities on the involvement of fan communities for their development and experiential value. As developments in advergaming indicate, indiscrete cultural commodities can be highly intertextual. Games are often developed as extensions of content brands. Game environments are also used as advertising and cross-promotion media. However, expert games producers do not fully determine the qualities of the computer game. Furthermore, the development costs and risks of commercial games development are now so prohibitively expensive that it is no longer feasible for games developers to proceed without extensive co-creative involvement of players (Banks 2002; Humphreys 2005; Jenkins 2006). The imperative to ensure market success is another reason why these risks are routinely managed by involving expert consumers in the games development process from the outset.

Like the intertextual commodity, digitization has facilitated the growth of indiscrete cultural commodities. Unlike the intertextual commodity, which has proliferated following the global consolidation of media and entertainment industries, the indiscrete commodity emerges from distributed, networked processes of knowledge and cultural production. The internet provides the archetype for the mode of conversationally-enabled knowledge production, which is characteristic of the innovation communities that computer games developers actively seek to cultivate as part of the games development process (Banks 2002; Humphreys 2005; Jenkins 2006). The end-to-end design principles of the early internet favoured its use as an open platform for harnessing distributed, collective intelligence (Lessig 2002). The possibilities for co-creative knowledge production and innovation that the intercreative communicative functionality of the internet enables are what make the internet a core infrastructure of the new economy. These features of the internet also underpin the emergence of innovation communities, exemplified by the successes of the free and open source software movement (Tuomi 2002).

Crucially, prevailing statutory approaches to copyright can have the effect of inhibiting the activities of innovation communities. An important enabler of co-creative productivity has been the development of alternative approaches to managing intellectual property. 'Copyleft' initiatives, such as the GNU General Public Licence pioneered by Richard Stallman (Stallman 2003), do not establish the market or social relations of information on the use of copyrights to leverage monopoly rents from the use of information goods. Instead, they create the conditions in which anyone can potentially share in the benefits of intellectual property. The GNU attached to the Linux operating system, for example, stipulates that anyone can copy, use and adapt the Linux source code for any purpose, including commercial purposes, as long as any adaptations remain available for others to use. Consequently, the Linux innovation community has grown exponentially, providing a perpetual and robust innovation system. Numerous businesses, small and large, now make their money from providing support services for Linux. Many others reduce their operating costs by using it. Because it remains cheap, world-wide adoption and diffusion of Linux is now so widespread that Linux is second only to Microsoft in terms of overall market share. Alternative copyright regimes developed to suit the needs of free and open source software communities. More recently, Lawrence Lessig has spearheaded the Creative Commons, a scheme designed to support the productivity of innovation communities of content creators.[1] Creative Commons licences do not aim to replace copyright. They aim to augment it by allowing creators to specify the uses that can be made of copyrighted works. Indeed, the EepyBird Coke–Mentos experiments, discussed in Chapter 1, were released under a Creative Commons licence that authorized their dissemination and reproduction across the Web.

As media and entertainment businesses seek to adapt the advertising-funded business model to the new economies of information and networks, important questions arise about their ambivalent relationship to innovation communities of content creators. These are, after all, powerful copyright industries with substantial stakes in extending and strengthening statutory copyright protections. Their interests in copyright run directly counter to those of innovations communities, which thrive where open, rather than exclusive, approaches to intellectual property prevail. In many respects, MySpace exhibits the qualities of a peer-to-peer marketing innovation community as well as an indiscrete cultural commodity dependent on the affective labour of community members. The acquisition of MySpace by News Corporation opens a series of important questions about the capacity of major stakeholders in the copyright industries to fairly and equitably manage the conflicting interests in copyright that inevitably arise. For example, can the innovation community potential of MySpace develop under these conditions? Is it possible for media and entertainment conglomerates to manage the production of both intertextual and indiscrete commodities? To what extent will their futures as media entities be dependent on managing this juggling act? Or do they become little more than content brand farms and marketing platforms? The example of computer games clearly suggests that it is possible for both strategies to co-exist, and that human tendencies to compete, collaborate, cluster and to seek recognition (Herz 2005) can be profitably leveraged in proprietary space.

Commercial media generally need to routinely re-make themselves as 'new' if they are to remain viable. In the digital media context, this means they need to diversify the ways in which they enable interaction with, and between, consumer markets and advertising clients. The classification of digital media, as popularized by Tim O'Reilly, into Web 1.0 and 2.0 is more helpful than the 'old'/'new' dichotomy (O'Reilly 2005). Descriptors such as 'old' or 'new' often prove to be clumsy and imprecise. The propositions of Web 1.0 and 2.0 business models seek to explain the success stories of internet-based media and e-commerce. Web 2.0 firms are built on, and make use of, network and information economics, conversational interaction and intercreative innovation. At the heart of their success are the principles of network interoperability and openness that support the formation of innovation communities around them. Web 1.0 seeks to describe those firms that persist with industrial modes of production and organization, and 'push' or transmission orientations to communication and distribution. Although Web 1.0 was initially coined to describe 'old' media approaches to 'new' media and communications platforms, it is sufficiently broad to generally accommodate 'old' offline as well as online media.

The discourses of and about the O'Reilly's scheme tend to valorize Web 2.0 strategies for delivering a superior alignment of commercial, consumer and wider public interests than Web 1.0 media. They are highly suggestive of new strategies for civilizing capital, which is an important part of their appeal in academic studies of new media. However, the O'Reilly scheme is not intended to support critical historical insight. For example, it would be a mistake to use it to periodize the historical development of the internet because it is only concerned with the commercialization of the Web. As such, it erases the pre-commercial history of the internet. Schemes such as that proposed by Graham Meikle (2002) of Internet 1.0, 2.0 and (by inference) 3.0, are much more useful for this purpose. Internet 1.0 describes the pre-commercial period of the internet; Internet 2.0 describes the early commercial period of the Internet, and encompasses the Web 1.0 phenomenon; and Internet 3.0 describes the maturation of internet-based media and e-commerce, including the articulation of the Web 2.0 philosophy. Web 2.0, nevertheless, provides an extremely useful frame of analysis for thinking through the implications of conversational interaction for commercial media and e-commerce.

The influence of Web 2.0 thinking on adaptive decision-making is reflected in acquisitions of Web 2.0 media by historically Web 1.0 media. While acquisition is easy enough where capital is plentiful, the challenges of integrating Web 2.0 properties into principally Web 1.0 business cultures seem significant, as the preceding discussion of News Corporation's acquisition of MySpace suggests. News Corporation looks increasingly like a content brand specialist, and content brands are built on exclusive proprietary approaches to managing intellectual property. The indiscrete social networks and products of innovation communities that new, Web 2.0 media businesses are built on can be managed proprietarily, but also rely on (indeed favour) non-exclusive approaches to intellectual property.

Importantly, media companies that are seeking to make the transition from mass to 'my' media markets do not have a monopoly on adaptation strategies. As new commercial media mature, they are compelled to embark on programmes of perpetual innovation in order to remain competitive in conversational media. Corporations – from AOL to Yahoo! and Google – rely on many, if not all of the market adaptation strategies identified by Pavlik. They also deploy a variety of business models in an effort to diversify revenue streams. In its merger with Time Warner, AOL secured access to an extensive cable infrastructure and content library. Ultimately, however, the opportunities for vertical integration were not as extensive or as immediately lucrative as the merger initially indicated. Yahoo! and Google have also applied the vast fortunes they have amassed in an incredibly short period of time to developing new services and applications, either in-house or through acquisitions strategies. This includes the acquisition of social networks, for example, Flickr by Yahoo! and YouTube by Google.

Far from disrupting the social relations of commercial media, Dwayne Winseck argues that the 'netscapes of power' established by 'old media' are proving to be quite resilient, and that commercial digital media are being recast 'in their image' (Winseck 2003: 180). These comments were made in the wake of the AOL–Time Warner merger and focus on the negative implications of digital networked media for diversity. Winseck nevertheless points to some important continuities of 'old' and 'new' media. Like mass media, new media corporations use network architecture to regulate behaviour. As David Marshall observes, 'the new media apparatus is highly structured and, through its very design, provides the range of possible choices in advance' (Marshall 2004: 17). The commercial media imperative to maintain advertising revenues will continue to be an important factor that shapes consumer interaction with commercial media enterprises into the future. The incentives for media and entertainment conglomerates to become marketing agents are strong but also limited by their ability to provide fully integrated solutions for advertisers. Advertisers will remain loyal to the mission of connecting with consumers, wherever they happen to be.

Notes

1 Advertising and the new media of mass conversation

1 'Extreme Diet Coke and Mentos Experiments' and other works by EepyBird, can be found on many websites including: Revver (http://one.revver.com/find/user/Eepybird); and YouTube (www.youtube.com/results?search_query=Eepybird&search=Search); and EepyBird's own website (www.eepybird.com).
1 For example, Adrants (2006) 'Mentos Loves Diet Coke, Coke Could Care Less', available at: http://www.adrants.com/2006/06/mentos-loves-diet-coke-coke-could-care-le.php (accessed 14 November 2006).
3 Many early internet advertising forms have since been rehabilitated by creative digital specialists. See, for example, London agency Profero's 'Follow the White Rabbit' campaign for BMW Mini at Cool Hunting (www.coolhunting.com/archives/2006/08/mini_white_rabb.php) and case study at Profero (www.profero.co.uk/uk/work.html).
4 See, for example, see the list of Web 2.0 publications maintained on the twopointouch blog, available at: http://twopointouch.com/2006/10/31/10-free-ebooks-about-web-20 (accessed 10 August 2007).

2 From the 'Long Tail' to 'Madison and Vine': trends in advertising and new media

1 Another innovative viral campaign, 'avaword', was developed for BMW Mini Cooper by glue London in 2006. Made to appeal to the UK 'lad' market, the campaign enabled visitors to the 'avaword' website to personalize a humorous, high quality audiovisual commercial message for individual friends using 'cutting edge interactive video techniques' (see www.gluelondon.com/casestudy.php?id=10).
2 The websites for any of the 100 or more territories in which the company operates can be accessed from www.coca-cola.com/index-d.html
3 See Shoehacker (2006) 'Nike+ IPod Sports Shoe Mod', Podophile Blog Archive. Available at: http://podophile.com/2006/07/14/shoe-hacker-nikeipod-sport-kit-shoe-mod (accessed 23 March 2007).
4 Information on Habbo Hotels is sourced from a presentation by CEO of Sulake Australia, Jeff Brooks, to the iMAT – Interactive Marketing and Trends conference, 18–19 August 2005, Sofitel Wentworth Hotel, Sydney, Australia.

3 Integrating interactivity: globalization and the gendering of creative advertising

1 French, N. (*c*. 2006) The Neilfrench Site. Available at: www.neilfrench.com/apology/index.html (accessed 8 May 2006).
2 Frank Mort (1996: 115) discusses UK research by Kitty O'Hagen which, in 1986, pointed to 'a widening gulf between the world view of a predominantly masculine profession and the consumer expectations of the majority of women. . . . Television soap operas had kept pace with these shifts far more effectively than advertising', with the result that many campaigns intended for women, 'missed their target by miles'.
3 Information about Unilever has been obtained from a variety of sources including the Unilever Corporate website (www.unilever.com); Adbrands (*c*. 2005) 'Unilever (UK/Netherlands)'. Available at: www.mind-advertising.com/nl/unilever_nl.htm (accessed 15 December 2005).
4 The facts of the Axe/Lynx case are drawn from a number of industry sources, including a presentation by Simon Sherwood, Chief Operating Officer, Bartle Bogle Hegarty, to the 39th congress of the International Advertising Association, Beijing, 10 September 2004, on 'The Global Creative Process: campaigns that exceed expectations'; Adforum (*c*. 2005) 'Tribal Women'. Available at: www.adforum.com/adfolio/reel_detail.asp?ID=25726&TDI=VDb6lEiK&PAGE=2&awid=(accessed 4 June 2006); and Adforum (*c*. 2005) 'Case Study: Pearl, Lever Faberge', available at: www.adforum.com/adfolio/reel_detail.asp?ID=51900&TDI=VDWu0hGK&PAGE=1&bShop=False&awcat=&ob=intlevel&awid=&wtype=film (accessed 13 December 2005); and campaign profiles such as Anon (2003a) 'Marketing Achievement – Winner', *Marketing*, June 2003: 20; and British Design and Art Direction (*c*. 2004) 'Lynx Pulse', Creativity Works case study, available at: www.dandad.org/inspiration/creativityworks/4/cases.html (accessed 20 December 2005).
5 The 'Make Luv' TVC can be viewed at Visit4info, Lynx Range, Lynx Pulse details, available at: www.visit4info.com/watchad.cfm?id=7658&type=coolad (accessed 20 December 2005).
6 The facts of the Dove case have been obtained from various industry sources, including the following resource from the Dove product website: 'Only Two Percent of Women Describe Themselves as Beautiful. New global study uncovers desire for broader definition of beauty', *Media Release*, 29 September 2004, available at: www.dove.com/real_beauty/news.asp?id=566 (accessed 13 December 2005); and the following resources from the Unilever corporate website: Unilever (2005) 'Real results for real women', available at: www.unilever.com/ourbrands/personalcare/dove.asp (accessed 13 December 2005); and Unilever (2005) Dove 'Key facts', available at: www.unilever.com/ourbrands/personalcare/dove.asp (accessed: 13 December 2005).
7 These examples of the debate stimulated by the repositioning of Dove come from the following blogs: R. Traister (2005) '"Real Beauty" – or really smart marketing?' Salon.com, 22 July 2005. Available at: www.salon.com/mwt/feature/2005/07/22/dove (accessed 13 December 2005); L. Top, (*c*. 2005) 'Dove Soap's "Real Beauty" Campaign', and 'Readers Comments', *AdJab.com*. Available at: www.adjab.com/, 2005/07/18/dove-soaps-real-beauty-campaign (accessed 13 December 2005); and Caffeinegoddess (2005) 'Embracing Real Beauty (part 2)', *Adland*. Available at: http://ad-rag.com/117085.php (accessed 13 December 2005).
8 Dove (2005) 'Only Two Percent of Women Describe Themselves as Beautiful. New global study uncovers desire for broader definition of beauty', *Media Release*, 29

September 2004, available at: www.dove.com/real_beauty/news.asp?id=566 (accessed 13 December 2005).

4 Mobilizing the local: advertising and cell phone industries in China

1 Facts about the Ningbo Bird case are drawn from a variety of industry sources including from the Nigbo Bird corporate website, (*c*. 2004) 'R&D' and 'World coverage'. Ningbo Bird International corporate website, available at: www.birdintl.com/worldwide.html (accessed 6 June 2005); PCBP case study materials; and a personal interview with PCBP Chairnan, Wu Xiaobo.

5 From conversation to registration: regulating advertising and new media

1 The facts of Jamster and 'The Crazy Frog' are publicly available from numerous sources and have been very helpfully consolidated in the Wikipedia: http://en.wikipedia.org/wiki/Crazy_Frog
2 For example, in 2005 Jamster introduced 'Jamster Guardian', a service that allows consumers to block access to Jamster premium rate mobile content services (www.order.amster.co.uk/jow/guardian/blockuser.do). See also, Tim Richardson, 'Jamster! lets parents take control', *The Register*, 19 September 2005. Available at: www.theregister.co.uk/2005/09/19/jamster_controls (accessed 24 August 2007).
3 See, for example, Jamster Scam, available at: www.jamsterscam.com (accessed 31 March 2007); Stop Jamster, available at: www.petitiononline.com/0wnj4m/petition.html (accessed 31 March 2007); ComWreck, available at: www.petitiononline.com/0wnj4m/petition.html (accessed 31 March 2007); and Blagger, available at: www.blagger.com/db4/company_id/1229/companyname/Jamster.html (accessed 31 March 2007).

6 The future of advertising-funded media

1 See www.creativecommons.org

References

Adegoke, Y. (2006) 'Long-tailed niche market where less is more', *Marketing Week*, 27 July: 24–25. Via Factiva (accessed 14 November 2006).

Advertising Federation of Australia (AFA) (2005) 'AFA Survey Shows Upturn in Employment and More Women in Senior Management', *Media Release*, November.

Ahmed, T. and Oppenheim, C. (2006) 'Experiments to Identify the Causes of Spam', *Aslib Proceedings*, 58(3): 156.

Anderson, C. (2004) 'The Long Tail', *Wired Magazine*, 12.10 (October). Available at: www.wired.com/wired/archive/12.10/tail.html (accessed 25 November 2006).

Anon (2003) 'Solicitous of Solicitors', *Multinational Monitor*, 24(10): 4.

—— (2005) 'A Rose by any Other Name?', *Communications of the ACM*, 48(7): 10.

—— (2006a) 'Advertising body fights click fraud', *IT Week*, August 14: 13.

—— (2006b) 'Beware of Click Fraud if you Count on Paid Search Engine Links for Sales Prospects', *The Kiplinger Letter*, 83(14): 1.

—— (2006c) 'Second Defendant Pleads Guilty in Prosecution of Major International Spam Operation', *Computer and Internet Lawyer*, 23(4): 31.

Ante, S., Yang, C. and Elgin, B. (2005) 'Sptizer's Spreading Spyware Net', *Business Week Online*, 5 May. Available at: www.businessweek.com/technology/content/may2005/tc2005055_1258_tc024.htm (accessed 14 April 2007).

Arens, W. F. (2002) *Contemporary Advertising* (8th edition), New York: McGraw-Hill.

Arora, V. (2006) 'The CAN-SPAM Act: An Inadequate Attempt to Deal with a Growing Problem', *Columbia Journal of Law and Social Problems*, 39(3): 299.

Arvidsson, A. (2006) *Brands. Meaning and Value in Media Culture*. London: Routledge.

Audit Bureau of Verification Services (ABVS) (2005) 'Online Advertising Market Grows Revenue to $488 Million', Media Release, 6 September, ABVS. Available at: www.auditbureau.org.au/ABC/info_resource/frame.html (accessed 23 September 2005).

Australian Broadcasting Commission (ABC) (2004) 'China's Mobile Phone Wars', *The Buzz*, Radio National programme transcript, first broadcast 7 August. Available at: www.abc.net.au/rn/science/stories/s1170716.htm (accessed 6 June 2005).

Awad, N. and Fitzgerald, K. (2005) 'The Deceptive Behaviors that Offend us Most about Spyware', *Communications of the ACM*, 48(8): 55–60.

Banks, J. (2002) 'Gamers and Co-Creators: Enlisting the Virtual Audience – A Report from the Net Face', in M. Balnaves, T. O'Regan, and J. Sternberg (eds), *Mobilizing the Audience*, St. Lucia: University of Queensland Press.

Battelle, John (2005) *The Search. How Google and its Rivals Rewrote the Rules of Business and Transformed our Culture*, New York: Penguin Group.

Bellovin, S. M. (2004) 'Spamming, Phishing, Authentication, and Privacy', *Communications of the ACM*, 47(12): 144.

Benady, A. (2005) 'John Hegarty: Master of Creative Rebellion', *The Independent*, (online edition) 10 November 2005 (accessed 13 December 2005).

Benkler (2006) *The Wealth of Networks. How Social Production Transforms Markets and Freedom*, New Haven, CT: Yale University Press.

Berghel, H. (2006) 'Phishing Mongers and Posers', *Communications of the ACM*, 49(4): 21–5.

Berman, C., Fedewa, D. and Caggiano, J. (2006) 'Still Miss Understood: She's not Buying your Ads', *Advertising & Society Review*, 7(2).

Berner, Robert and Kiley, David (2005) 'Global Brands', Annual Report, *Business Week*, 1 August, 86–94.

Berry, M. (1998) *The New Integrated Direct Marketing*, Aldershot, Hampshire: Gower.

Blackshaw, P. and Nazzaro, M. (2004) 'Consumer-Generated Media (CGM) 101: Word of Mouth is the Ace of the Web-Fortified Consumer,' Intelliseek White Paper. Available at: www. intelliseek.com/whitepapers.asp (accessed 25 November 2006).

Blankenhorn, D. (2006) 'Corruption on the Web', *Moore's Lore*, 2 February, available at: http://mooreslore.corante.com/archives/2006/02/02/corruptions_on_the_web.php (accessed 17 February 2007).

Bond, J. and Kirshenbawm, R. (1998) *Under the Radar. Talking to Today's Cynical Consumer*, New York: John Wiley & Sons.

Bordewijk, J. L. and van Kaam, B. (2003) 'Towards a New Classification of Tele-Information Services,' in N. Wardrip-Fruin and N. Montfort (eds) *The New Media Reader*, Cambridge, MA: MIT Press.

Boslet, M. (2006) 'Web Advertising, Version 2.0: Cost-Per-Action Model is Studied', *Wall Street Journal*, 21 September, B2D.

Brecht, B. (1979) 'Radio as a Means of Communication: A Talk on the Function of Radio', S. Hood (trans.), *Screen*, 20(3/4), Winter: 24–8.

Brown, J. and Duguid, P. (2002) *The Social Life of Information*, Boston, MA: Harvard Business School Publishing.

Bruno, L. (2003) 'Baffling the Bots', *Scientific American*, 289(5): 36–8.

Bruns, Axel and Jacobs, Joanne (2006) *Uses of Blogs*, New York: Peter Lang.

Burnett, R. and Marshall, P. D. (2003) *Web Theory. An Introduction*, London: Routledge.

Canning, S. (2005) 'How to Get Creative Rise out of Women', Media and Marketing Supplement, *The Australian*, 27 October, p. 19.

Cappo, J. (2003) *The Future of Advertising. New Media, New Clients, New Consumers in the Post-television Age*, New York: McGraw-Hill.

Carey, J. (1992) *Communication as Culture. Essays on Media and Society*, London: Routledge.

Castells, M. (2002) *The Internet Galaxy. Reflections on the Internet, Business, and Society*, Oxford: Oxford University Press.

Cerf, V. (2005) 'Spam, Spim, and Spit', *Communications of the Association for Computing Machinery*, 48(4): 39.

Chabrow, E. (2005) 'In the Fight against Spam, a Few Knockouts', *InformationWeek*, (1052): 34.

Chang, J., Wan, I. and Qu, P. (eds) (2003) *China's Media and Entertainment Law*, TransAsia, Price Waterhouse Coopers.

China Advertising Association (CAA) (2003) *Annual Industry Report*. Available at: www. china-aa.org/second/en/main.asp (accessed 28 January 2004).

Cleland, K. (2000) 'Addressable Advertising a Matter of Time', *Advertising Age*, 71(15): S24.

Clendenin, M. (2004) 'China's Handset Makers Prepare to Call Overseas', *CommsDesign*, 26 July. Available at: www.commsdesign.com/showArticle.jhtml?articleID=25600137 (accessed 6 June 2005).

Consumers' Telecommunications Network (CTN) (2006) *Surfing on Thin Ice. Consumers and Adware, Malware, Spam and Phishing*, Sydney: CTN.

Cronin, A. (2000) *Advertising and Consumer Citizenship*, London: Routledge.

—— (2004) *Advertising Myths. The Strange Half-lives of Images and Commodities*, London: Routledge.

Cunningham, S. (1992) *Framing Culture. Criticism and Policy in Australia*, North Sydney: Allen & Unwin.

Daniels, P. (1997) *Advertising Services in an Era of Open International Markets. Changing Roles of State Intervention in Services in an Era of Open International Markets,* Aharoni, Y. (ed.), Albany, NY: State University of New York Press.

Davidson, M. (1992) *The Consumerist Manifesto. Advertising in Postmodern Times*, London: Routledge.

Davis, H. and Scase, R. (2000) *Managing Creativity. The Dynamics of Work and Organization*, Buckingham: Open University Press.

DeMarco, D. (2006) 'Understanding Consumer Information Privacy in the Realm of Internet Commerce: Personhood and Pragmatism, Pop-Tarts and Six-Packs', *Texas Law Review*, 84(4): 1013.

Dettmer, R. (2003) 'Wham, Bam – You've got Spam', *IEE Review*, 49(8): 38.

Dickinson, D. (2004) 'An Architecture for Spam Regulation', *Federal Communications Law Journal*, 57(1): 129.

Donald, S., Keane, M. and Hong, Y. (eds) (2002) *Media in China. Consumption, Content and Crisis*, London: RoutledgeCurzon.

Donaton, S. (2004) *Madison and Vine. Why the Entertainment and Advertising Industries must Converge to Survive*, New York: McGraw-Hill.

Downes, E. and McMillan, J. (2000) 'Defining Interactivity: A qualitative identification of key dimensions', *New Media & Society*, 2(2): 157–79.

Dunn, A. (2003) 'Ethics Impossible? Advertising and the Infomercial', in C. Lumby and E. Probyn (eds) *Remote Control: New Media, New Ethics*, Victoria: Cambridge University Press.

Eaton, M. (2004) 'Sponsors Ready to Party', *Ad News* (online) 7 May. Available at: www.adnews.com.au/archives_detail.cfm?ArticleID=16117 (accessed 21 April 2007).

Einhorn, B. (2003) 'How Ningbo Bird Became a High-Flier', *Business Week Online*, 21 January. Available at: www.businessweek.com/technology/content/jan2003/tc30020121_7804.htm (accessed 6 June 2005).

Elkin, T. (2005) 'Just One Minute', *Media Post*, 30 September. Available at: http://publications.mediapost.com/index.cfm?fuseaction=Articles.showArticle&art_aid=34694 (accessed 13 October 2005).

eMarketer (2007) 'Social Network Marketing, February 2007', IAB. Available at: www.iab.net/resources/industrystats.asp (accessed 22 March 2007).

Enzensberger (1974) *The Consciousness Industry. On Literature, Politics and the Media*, New York: Seabury Press.

Federal Trade Commission (FTC) (2005a) *Email Address Harvesting and the Effectiveness of Anti-Spam Filters*, FTC.

—— (2005b) *The US Safe Web Act. Protecting Consumers from Spam, Spyware and Fraud*, FTC.

Flew, T. (2002; 2nd edition 2005) *New Media. An Introduction*, Melbourne: Oxford University Press.

Ford, R. (2005) 'Preemption of State Spam Laws by the Federal CAN-SPAM Act', *The University of Chicago Law Review*, 72(1): 355.

Fox, S. (1997) *The Mirror Makers. A History of American Advertisers and Its Creators*, Urbana, IL: University of Illinois Press.

Frank, T. (1997) *The Conquest of Cool*, Chicago, IL: University of Chicago Press.

Frith, K. T. and Meuller, B. (2003) *Advertising and Societies. Global Issues*, New York: Peter Lang Publishing.

Galician, M.-L. (ed.) (2004) *Handbook of Product Placement in the Mass Media. New Strategies in Marketing Theory, Practice, Trends, and Ethics*, Binghamton, NY: Best Business Books.

Gallagher, B. (2004) 'BFE Way to Viewer Hear', *Ad News* (online), 1 July. Available at: www.adnews.com.au/archives_detail.cfm?ArticleID=1440 (accessed 21 April 2007).

Gandy, O. (1993) *The Panoptic Sort. A Political Economy of Personal Information*, Boulder, CO: Westview.

Gates, B. (1996) *The Road Ahead*, New York: Penguin.

Gawlinski, M. (2003) *Interactive Television Production*, Oxford: Focal Press.

Gelman, R. and McCandlish, S. (1998) *Protecting Yourself Online. The Definitive Resource on Safety, Freedom, and Privacy in Cyberspace*, New York: HarperEdge HarperCollins.

Gelston, S. (2005) 'Make a Campaign Happen despite Senior Management', CMO Perspectives 2005. Available at: www.cmomagazine.com/conferences/05_perspectives/hayden.html (accessed 20 December 2005).

Gershman, A. and Fano, A. (2006) 'Ubiquitous Services: Extending Customer Relationship Management', in G. Roussos (ed.) *Ubiquitous and Pervasive Commerce. New Frontiers for Electronic Business*, London: Springer-Verlag.

Gerth, K. (2003) *China Made. Consumer Culture and the Creation of the Nation*, Cambridge, MA: Harvard University Asia Centre.

Gill, R. (2002) 'Cool, Creative and Egalitarian? Exploring Gender in Project-based New Media Work in Europe', *Information, Communication & Society*, 5(1): 70–89.

Gladwell, M. (2002) *The Tipping Point*, Boston, MA: Back Bay Books.

Goggin, G. (2006) *Cell Phone Culture. Mobile Technology in Everyday Life*, London: Routledge.

Goggin, G. and Spurgeon, C. (2007) 'Premium Rate Culture: The New Business of Mobile Interactivity', *New Media & Society* (forthcoming, October 2007, Issue 9(5)).

Gogoi, P. (2005) 'From Reality TV to Reality Ads', *Business Week*, 17 August 2005. Available at: www.businessweek.com/bwdaily/dnflash/aug2005/nf20050817_5273_db035.htm (accessed 13/12/05).

Goldman, E. (2006) 'Datamining and Attention Consumption', in K. Strandburg and D. Raicu (eds) *Privacy and Technologies of Identity. A Cross-Disciplinary Conversation*, New York: Springer.

Goldsborough, R. (2006) 'The End of the Free Internet?', *Office Solutions*, 23(5): 51.

Google (2004) *Securities and Exchange Commission Registration Statement*, Google Inc., 18 August, p. 51. Available at: www.sec.gov/Archives/edgar/data/1288776/00011931 2504142742/ds1a.htm#toc59330_11 (accessed 4 September 2005).

—— (2006) 'Google to Acquire YouTube for $1.65 Billion in Stock', Press Release, 9 October. Available at: www.google.com/press/pressrel/google_youtube.html (accessed 22 March 2007).

Gould, L. (2007) 'Cash and Controversy: A Short History of Commercial Talkback Radio', *Media International Australia*, No. 122 (February): 81–95.

Graham, P. (2006) *New Media, Language and Social Perceptions of Value*, New York: Peter Lang.

Greenspan, B. (2006) *MySpace Report*. Available at: http://freemyspace.com/?page_id=12 (accessed 14 April 2007).

Gross, G. (2005) 'U.S. CAN-SPAM Act Struggles to Make a Difference', *InfoWorld*, 27(1): 16.

Grow, B. and Elgin, B. with Herbst, M. (2006) 'Click Fraud', *Business Week* (4003): 46.

Hanseel, S. (2006) 'Postage is Due for Companies Sending E-Mail', NYTimes.com, 5 February. Available at: www.nytimes.com/2006/02/05/technology/05AOL.html?ex = 1171861200&en = cfe7d19e2dfcbefb&ei = 5070 (accessed 17/2/07).

Harris, R. (2007) *Film in the Age of Digital Distribution. The Challenge for Australian Content*, Sydney: Currency House.

Hartley, J. (1999) *Uses of Television*, London: Routledge.

Hartley, J. (ed.) (2005) *Creative Industries*, Malden, MA: Blackwell.

Hartley, J. (2007) '"Reality" and the Plebescite', in K. Riegert (ed.) *Politicotainment. Television's Take on the Real*, New York: Peter Lang.

Herman, E. and McChesney, R. (1997) *The Global Media. The New Missionaries of Global Capitalism*, London: Cassell.

Herz, J. C. (2005) 'Harnessing the Hive', in J. Hartley (ed.) *Creative Industries*, Massachusetts: Blackwell.

Hesmondhalgh, D. (2002) *The Cultural Industries*, London: Sage.

Hill, R. and Dhanda, K. (2002) 'Advertising, Technology and the Digital Divide', in C. Taylor (ed.) *New Directions in International Advertising Research*, Amsterdam: JAI.

Hirsch, D. (2006) 'Is Privacy Regulation the Environmental Law of the Information Age?', in K. Strandburg and D. Raicu (eds) *Privacy and Technologies of Identity. A Cross-Disciplinary Conversation*, New York: Springer.

Ho, A., Kwan, P., Kwong, K. and Or, R. (1997) *The Effects of Corporate Images Built through Celebrity Advertising on Consumers' Attitudes, Choice Sets and Purchase Decisions – A Case Study of Hong Kong Mobile Communications Industry*. Available at, http://home.netvigator.com/~kwongkf/4060pg01.htm (accessed on 24 June 2004).

Hood, J. (2005) *Selling the Dream. Why Advertising is Good Business*, Westport, CT: Praeger.

Hove, J. (2005) 'The Hit Factory', *Wired*, Issue 13.11, November. Available at: www.wired.com/wired/archive/13.11/myspace.html (accessed 14 April 2007).

Howkins, J. (2001) *The Creative Economy. How People Make Money From Ideas*, London: The Penguin Group.

Hu, Q. and Dinev, T. (2005) 'Is Spyware an Internet Nuisance or Public Menace?', *Communications of the ACM*, 48(8): 61–6.

Huang, S. and Chen, S. (2004) 'Report on the Development of China's Advertising Industry from 2002–3', in Zhang Xiaoming, Hu Huilin and Zhang Jiangang (eds) *Development Report on China's Cultural Industries: 2004*, Shanghai: Social Sciences Documentation Publishing House.

Humphreys, S. (2005) 'Productive Users, Intellectual Property and Governance: the Challenges of Computer Games', *Media and Arts Law Review*, 10(4): 299–310.

Hunter, R. (2002) *World Without Secrets*, New York: John Wiley & Sons.

Illich, I. (1985) *Tools for Conviviality*, London: Marion Boyars Publishers.

Institute of Practitioners in Advertising (IPA) (2004) 'Agency Census 2003: A Report on IPA Member Agencies', February. Available at: www.ipa.co.uk/news/news_archive/displayitem.cfm?ItemID=1140 (accessed 8 December 2005).

Interactive Advertising Bureau (IAB) UK (2006) *Fact Sheet: Online Adspend – First Half 2006*. Available at: www.iabuk.net/en/1/iabknowledgebankadspendadspendfct-shth12006.html (accessed 22 March 2006).

International Telecommunications Union (ITU) (2002) 'Asia's Biggest Growth is Yet to Come: Telecommunications Epicentre Shifting to Asia-Pacific Region', Press Release, 2 December. Available at: www.itu.int/newsarchive/press_releases/2002/32.html (accessed 24 June 2004).

Jaffe, A. (2003) *Casting for Big Ideas. A New Manifesto for Agency Managers*, New Jersey: John Wiley & Sons.

Jenkins, H. (2003) 'Digital Cinema: Media Convergence, and Participatory Culture', in D. Thorburn and H. Jenkins (eds) *Rethinking Media Change. The Aesthetics of Transition*, Cambridge, MA: The MIT Press.

—— (2006) *Convergence Culture. Where Old and New Media Collide*, London: New York University Press.

Jensen, J. F. (1999) 'Interactivity – Tracking a New Concept in Media and Communication Studies,' in P. Mayer, (ed.) *Computer Media and Communication. A Reader*, Oxford: Oxford University Press.

Jhally, S. (1990) *The Codes of Advertising. Fetishism and the Political Economy of Meaning in the Consumer Society*, New York: Routledge.

—— (2002) 'Image-Based Culture: Advertising and Popular Culture', in K. Askew and R. Wilks (eds) *The Anthropology of Media*, Malden, MA: Blackwell.

Johnsson, J. (2004) 'Uh-Oh, Ningbo', *Crain's Chicago Business*, 25 April. Available at: www.tbri.com/News/pgViewArticle.asp?Id=273 (accessed 6 June 2005).

Kalehoff, M. (2005) 'A Google Scenario', *Search Insider*, 8 September. Available at: http://publications.mediapost.com/index.cfm?fuseaction=Articles.showArticle&art_aid=33887 (accessed 14 September 2005).

Keane, M. (2007) *Created in China. The Great New Leap Forward*, London: RoutledgeCurzon.

Keane, M. and Spurgeon, C. (2004) 'Advertising Industry and Culture in Post-WTO China', *Media International Australia*, No. 111 (May): 104–17.

—— (2005) 'Advertising Industries and China's Creative Vision'. Paper presented at AMIC Conference, 'Media & Society in Asia: Transformations and Transitions', Chinese University of Communication, Beijing, 18–21 July.

Klein, N. (2000) *No Logo. Taking Aim at the Brand Bullies*, London: Flamingo.

Kline, S., Dyer-Witherford, N. and De Peuter, G. (2003) *Digital Play. The Interaction of Technology, Culture and Marketing*, Montreal: McGill-Queen's University Press.

Kokernak, M. (2000) 'Fighting for Interactive', *Mediaweek*, 10(29): 26.

Lapinski, T. (2006) 'My Space: The Business of Spam 2.0 (Exhaustive Edition)', *Valleywag*, 11 September. Available at: http://valleywag.com/tech/myspace/myspace-the-business-of-spam-20-exhaustive-edition-199924.php (accessed 14 April 2007).

Lee, Eric (2005) *How Internet Radio Can Change the World. An Activist's Handbook*, New York: iUniverse.

Leiss, W., Kline, S. and Jhally, S. (1997) *Social Communication in Advertising* (2nd edition), London: Routledge.

Leiss, W., Kline, S., Jhally, S. and Botterill, J. (2005) *Social Communication in Advertising. Consumption in the Mediated Market Place* (3rd edition), London: Routledge.

Leo Burnett Worldwide (LBW) (2004) 'Leo Burnett Discovers Ads Aimed at Women Fall Short on Five Counts', Media Release 24 June. Available at: www.leoburnett.com/news/press_releases/2004/prjul09–13743.asp (accessed 7 December 2005).

Lessig, L. (1999) *Code and Other Laws of Cyberspace*, New York: Basic Books.

—— (2002) *The Future of Ideas. The Fate of the Commons in a Connected World*, New York: Vintage Books.

—— (2006) *Code 2.0*, New York: Basic Books.

Levitt, Theodore (1983) 'The Globalization of Markets', *Harvard Business Review*, 61 (May–June): 92–101.

Lim, M. (2003). 'The Internet, Social Networks, and Reform in Indonesia', in N. Couldry and J. Curran (eds) *Contesting Media Power. Alternative Media in a Networked World*, Oxford: Rowman & Littlefield.

Lininger, R. and Vines, R. (2005) *Phishing. Cutting the Identity Theft Line*, Indianapolis, IN: Wiley Publishing.

Locke, Christopher (2000) 'Internet Apocalyso', in R. Levine, C. Locke, C. Searles and D. Weinberger (2000) *The Cluetrain Manifesto. The End of Business as Usual*, Cambridge, MA: Perseus Books.

Luhmann, N. (2000) *The Reality of the Mass Media*, Cambridge: Polity Press.

Lynch, K. (1997) 'I went to the FTC spam hearing today (long)', Newsgroup post. Available at: http://keithlynch.net/ftc.html (accessed 3 February 2003).

Lyon, D. (2003). 'Surveillance as Social Sorting. Computer Codes and Mobile Bodies', in D. Lyon (ed.) *Surveillance as Social Sorting. Privacy, Risk, and Digital Discrimination*, London: Routledge.

McAllister, M. (1996) *Commercialization of American cultures. New Advertising, Control and Democracy*, Thousand Oaks, CA: Sage.

McCracken, G. (2005) *Culture and Consumption II. Markets, Meaning and Brand Management*, Bloomington, IN: Indiana University Press.

McFall, L. (2004) *Advertising: A Cultural Economy*, London: Sage.

McMillan, S. (2002) 'Exploring Models of Interactivity from Multiple Research Traditions: Users, Documents and Systems', in L. Lievrouw and S. Livingstone (eds) *The Handbook of New Media*, London: Sage.

Malefyt, T. de Waal (2006) 'The Privatization of Consumption: Marketing Media through Sensory Modalities', *Media International Australia*, 119 (May): 85–98.

Marketing Week (2006) 'Long tail niche market where less is more', 27 July. Via Factiva (accessed 14 November 2006).

Marshall, P. D. (2004) *New Media Cultures*, London: Arnold.

Mattelart, A. (2002) *Advertising International*, London: Routledge.

Maxwell, A. (2003) 'Women: Careers in Advertising', in J. McDonough *et al.* (eds) *Advertising Age Encyclopedia of Advertising*, New York: Fitzroy Dearborn (Vol. 3: 1655).

Meikle, G. (2002) *Future Active. Media Activism and the Internet*, New York: Routledge.

Messer, B. (2004) 'Don't Touch that Dial', *Ad News*, 30 July, p. 24.

MFC Insight (2003) *China's Mobile Data Market. On the Move!*, May, Beijing: MFC Insight.

Middleton, C. (2002) 'Exploring consumer demand for networked services: the importance of content, connectivity and killer apps in the diffusion of broadband and mobile services', paper presented at the *Twenty-third International Conference on Information*

Systems, 15–18 December, Barcelona, Spain. Available at: aisel.isworld.org/article_all.asp?Publication_ID=31 (accessed 22 October, 2005).

Moore, C. (1998) 'Behaving Outrageously: Contemporary Gay Masculinity', *Journal of Australian Studies*, No. 56: 158–68.

Morris, P. (1996) 'Newspapers and the New Information Media', *Media International Australia*, 79 (February): 11–21.

Mort, F. (1996) *Cultures of Consumption. Masculinities and Social Space in Late Twentieth-Century Britain*, London: Routledge.

Mosco, V. (1996) *The Political Economy of Communication*, London: Sage.

Mullin, R. (2002) *Direct Marketing*, London: Kogan Page.

Myers, K. (1986) *Understains. The Sense and Seduction of Advertising*, London: Comedia.

Negus, K. (2002) 'Identities and Industries: the Cultural Formation of Aesthetic Economies', in P. Du Gay and M. Pryke (eds) *Cultural Economy*, London: Sage.

News Corporation (2006) 'News Corporation and VeriSign Announce Joint Venture to Create Leading Global Mobile Entertainment Company', Press Release, 12 September. Available at: www.newscorp.com/news/news_312.html (accessed 11 April 2007).

Nightingale, V. and Dwyer, T. (2006) 'The Audience Politics of "Enhanced" Television Formats', *International Journal of Media and Cultural Politics*, 2(1): 23–42.

Nixon, S. (2003) *Advertising Cultures. Gender, Commerce, Creativity*, London: Sage.

Nolan, P. (2001) *China and the Global Economy, National Champions, Industrial Policy, and the Big Business Revolution*, Palgrave: Hampshire.

Ogilvy, D. (2004) *Confessions of an Advertising Man*, London: Southbank Publishing.

Olivier Recruitment Group (2002) *Internet Job Index, Full Report*, November. Available at: www.olivier.com.au (accessed 4 February 2003).

O'Regan, T. and Goldsmith, B. (2002) 'Emerging Global Ecologies of Production', in D. Harries (ed.) *The New Media Book*, London: British Film Institute.

O'Reilly, T. (2005) 'What is Web 2.0. Design Patterns and Business Models for the Next Generation of Software'. Available at: www.oreillynet.com/pub/a/oreilly/tim/news/2005/09/30/what-is-web-20.html (accessed 24 November 2006).

Oser, K. (2005) 'Marketers Fume over Click Fraud', *Advertising Age*, 76(11): 34.

Packard, V. (1960) *The Hidden Persuaders*, Ringwood, Vic.: Penguin Books.

Pavlik, J. (1998) *New Media Technology. Cultural and Commercial Perspectives*, Boston, MA: Allyn & Bacon.

Peiss, K. (1996) 'Making Up, Making Over: Cosmetics, Consumer Culture, and Women's Identity', in V. de Grazia and E. Furlough (eds) *The Sex of Things. Gender and Consumption in Historical Perspective*, Berkeley, CA: University of California Press.

Peppers, D. and Rogers, M. (1997) *Enterprise One To One. Tools for Competing in the Interactive Age*, New York: Currency/Doubleday.

Phillips, D. and Curry, M. (2003) 'Privacy and the Phenetic Urge: Geodemographics and the Changing Spatiality of Local Practice', in D. Lyon (ed.) *Surveillance as Social Sorting: Privacy, Risk, and Digital Discrimination*, London: Routledge.

Picard, R. (2000) 'Changing Business Models of Online Content Services', *JMM – The International Journal on Media Management*, 2(2): 60–8.

—— (2002) 'U.S. Newspaper Ad Revenue Shows Consistent Growth', *Newspaper Research Journal*, Fall: 21–33. Via Proquest (accessed 21 November 2003).

Prescott, L. (2006) 'Diet Coke and Mentos Expeiments – Brand Questions', Hitwise

Analyst Weblogs, 12 June. Available at: http://weblogs.hitwise.com/leeann-prescott/2006/06/diet_coke_and_mentos_experimen.html (accessed 14 November 2006).

PriceWaterHouseCoopers (PWC) (2005), *IAB Internet Advertising Revenue Report. 2004 Full Year Results*, Internet Advertising Bureau (US), available at: www.iab.net/resources/ad_revenue.asp (accessed 23 September 2005).

—— (2006) *IAB Internet Advertising Revenue Report. Full Year Results*, Internet Advertising Bureau (US). Available at: www.iab.net/resources/ad_revenue.asp (accessed 22 March 2007).

Quart, A. (2003) *Branded. The Buying and Selling of Teenagers*, London: Arrow, Random House Group.

Rakow, L. (1997) 'The Telephone and Women's Place', in S. Druckert and G. Gumpert (eds) *Voices in the Street. Explorations in Gender, Media, and Public Space*, Cresskill, NJ: Hampton Press.

Rao, M. (2005) 'Wireless and Mobile Impacts on News and Entertainment', in M. Rao and L. Mendoza (eds) *Asia Unplugged. The Wireless and Mobile Media Boom in the Asia Pacific*, New Delhi: Sage.

Raphael, J., Bacey, C. and Clark, K. (2003). 'Yellow Pages', in J. McDonough *et al.* (eds) *Advertising Age Encyclopedia of Advertising*, New York: Fitzroy Dearborn (Vol. 3: 1684–5).

Rayport, J. and B. Jaworski (2002) *Cases in e-Commerce*, Boston, MA: McGraw-Hill/Irwin.

Reid, R. (1997) *Architects of the Web. 1000 Days the Built the Future of Business*, New York: John Wiley & Sons.

Reiss, S. (2006) 'His Space', *Wired*, Issue 14.07, July. Available at: www.wired.com/wired/archive/14.07/murdoch.html?pg = 1&topic = murdoch&topic_set = (accessed 11 April 2007).

Rheingold, Howard (2002) *Smart Mobs. The Next Social Revolution*, Cambridge MA: Basic Books.

Roberts, M. (2001) 'Global Issues in Branding, Communication and Corporate Structure', in P. Kitchen and D. Schultz (eds) *Raising the Corporate Umbrella. Corporate Communication in the 21st Century*, New York: Palgrave.

Robertson, R. (1994). 'Globalisation or Glocalisation?', *Journal of International Communication*, 1(1): 33–52.

Rose, F. (2004) 'Hello Ningbo', *Wired*, Issue 12.04, April. Available at: www.wired.com/wired/archive/12.04/ningbo_pr.html (accessed 6 June 2004).

Rushkoff, D. (1994). *Media Virus. Hidden Agendas in Popular Culture*, New York: Ballantine Books.

Sainsbury, M. and Clow, R. (2006) 'Telstra Eyes Telecom NZ directories', *The Australian*, 31 August: 19.

Sandoval, G. (2006) 'Coke-and-Mentos Video Makers Get Google's Ad Dollar: Shake Your Money Maker', CNET News, 31 October. Via Factiva (accessed 14 November 2006).

Schudson, M. (1993) *Advertising, the Uneasy Persuasion*, London: Routledge.

Schulz, D. (1999). 'Integrated Marketing Communications and How It Relates to Traditional Media Advertising', in J. Jones (ed.) *The Advertising Business. Operations, Creativity, Media Planning, Integrated Communications*, Thousand Oaks, CA: Sage.

Sciadas, G. (ed.) (2005) *From the Digital Divide to Digital Opportunities. Measuring Infostates for Development*, Montreal: Orbicom-ITU. Available at: www.itu.int/ITU-D/ict/publications/dd/summary.html (accessed 22 April 2007).

Searles, D. (2000) 'Markets Are Conversations', in R. Levine, C. Locke, C. Searles and D. Weinberger (2000) *The Cluetrain Manifesto. The End of Business as Usual*, Cambridge, MA: Perseus Books.

Shukla, S. and Nah, F. (2005) 'Web Browsing and Spyware Intrusion', *Communications of the ACM*, 48(8): 85–90.

Sinclair, J. (1987) *Images Incorporated. Advertising Ad Industry and Ideology*, Kent: Croom Helm.

Sinclair, J. (ed.) (2004) *Contemporary World Television*, London: British Film Institute.

Sinclair, J. (2006) 'Globalisation Trends in Australia's Advertising Industry', *Media International Australia*, 119 (May): 112–23.

Sinclair, L. (2005) 'Google Irks Agencies with Ad Reward Plan', Media Supplement, *The Australian*, Thursday, 10 November, p. 17.

Slater, D. (2002) 'Capturing Markets from Economists', in P. Du Gay and M. Pryke (eds) *Cultural Economy*, London: Sage.

Smulyan, S. (1994) *Selling Radio. The Commercialization of American Broadcasting 1920–1934*, Washington, DC: Smithsonian Institution Press.

Smythe, D. (1981) *Dependency Road. Communications, Capitalism, Consciousness and Canada*, New York: Ablex.

Soar, M. (2000) 'Encoding Advertisements: Ideology and Meaning in Advertising Production', *Mass Communication & Society*, 3(4): 415–37.

Sokolov, A. (ed.) (2005) *Identity Theft on the Rise*, New York: Nova Science Publishers.

Sophocleous, A. (2003) 'Online Grows Up', *Ad News*, 21 November, pp. 27–8.

Spamhaus Project (2007) 'Register of Known Spam Operations'. Available at: www.spamhaus.org/rokso/index.lasso (accessed 10/2/2007).

Spangler, W., Hartzel, K. and Gal-Or, M. (2006) 'Exploring the Privacy Implications of Addressable Advertising and Viewer Profiling', *Communications of the ACM*, 49(5): 119.

Spender, D. (1995) *Nattering on the Net. Women, Power and Cyberspace*, Melbourne: Spinifex Press.

Spurgeon, C. (2003) 'Classified Advertising on the Move: Implications for Newspapers', *Australian Journalism Review*, 25(2): 51–62.

Spurgeon, C. and Goggin, G. (2007) 'Mobiles into Media: Premium Rate SMS and the Adaptation of Television to Interactive Communication Cultures', *Continuum* (in press).

Stafford, A. (2005) 'Privacy in Peril', *PC World*, 23(11): 101–4.

Steinem, G. (1994) 'Sex Lies and Advertising', in G. Steinem, *Moving Beyond Words*, New York: Simon & Schuster.

Stallman, R. (2003) 'The GNU Manifesto', in N. Wardrip-Fruin and N. Montfort, (eds) *The New Media Reader*, Cambridge MA: MIT Press.

Swartz, N. (2004) 'What Spam Law? Next up: Spim', *Information Management Journal*, 38(3): 12.

Tacchi, J. (2005) 'Supporting the Democratic Voice through Community Media Centres in South Asia', *3Cmedia: Journal of Community, Citizen's and Third Sector Media*, Issue 1 (February): 25–36. Available at: www.cbonline.org.au/3cmedia/3c_issue1/index.shtm (accessed 22 April 2007).

Tannos, S. (2003) 'Clients to the Rescue', *AdNews*, 24 October 2003, p. 16.

Telecommunications Industry Ombudsman & Banking and Financial Services Ombudsman (2005) *Sort It. Mobile Phone, Credit Card and Other Disputes*, Melbourne: TIO & B&FSO. Available at: www.tio.com.au/publications/SortIt.pdf (accessed 31 March 2007).

Telstra (2004) *Annual Report*, Available at: www.telstra.com.au/abouttelstra/investor/annual_reports.cfm?ReportDate=2004&ReportType=1 (accessed 6 September 2005).

Toffler, A. (1970) *Future Shock*, London: Bodley Head.

Tomlinson, A. (2002) 'The Many Benefits of Online Job Boards', *Canadian HR Reporter*, 15(13): 17–19.

Turner, E. S. (1965) *The Shocking History of Advertising*, Harmondsworth: Penguin Books.

Turner, G., Bonner, F. and Marshall, P. D. (2000) *Fame Games. The Products of Celebrity in Australia*, Cambridge: Cambridge University Press.

Turner, K. (2004) 'Insinuating the Product into the Message: An Historical Context for Product Placement', in M.-L. Galician (ed.) *Handbook of Product Placement in the Mass Media. New Strategies in Marketing Theory, Practice, Trends, and Ethics*, Binghamton, NY: Best Business Books.

Tuomi, I. (2002) *Networks of Innovation. Change and Meaning in the Age of the Internet*, New York: Oxford University Press.

Turow, J. (1997) *Breaking Up America*, Chicago, IL: University of Chicago Press.

—— (2000) 'Segmenting, Signalling and Tailoring: Probing the Dark Side of Target Marketing', in R. Andersen and L. Strate (eds) *Critical Studies in Media Commercialism*, Oxford: Oxford University Press.

Van Dijk (2006) *The Network Society. Social Aspects of New Media*, London: Sage.

van Duyn, A. and Waters, R. (2006) 'Google in $900m ad deal with MySpace', *FT.com*, August 7. Available at: www.ft.com/cms/s/17e8e67e-2660-11db-afa1–0000779e2340.html (accessed 22 March 2007).

Van Zoonen, L. (2002) 'Gendering the Internet. Claims, Controversies and Cultures', *European Journal of Communication*, 17(1): 5–23.

Varey, R. (2002) *Marketing Communication. Principles and practice*, London, New York: Routledge.

Veiner, A. (2005) 'Troubles at Google AdWords?', *GoYaMi*, Blog Post 21 April. Available at: www.corante.com/goyami/archives/2005/04/21/troubles_at_google_adwords.php (accessed 2 August 2005).

Vranica, S. and Terhune, C. (2006) 'Mixing Diet Coke and Mentos Makes a Gusher of Publicity', *Wall Street Journal*, June 12, Page B1. Available at: http://online.wsj.com/public/article/SB115007602216777497–1mzdx_pOFlMBwo9UAiqbsgY6MZ0_20060619.html?mod = blogs (accessed 14 November 2006).

Wall, D. (2004) 'Digital Realism and the Governance of Spam as Cybercrime', *European Journal on Criminal Policy and Research*, 10(4): 309–35.

Wang, J. (2003) 'China', in J. McDonough *et al.* (eds) *The Advertising Age Encyclopedia of Advertising*, Volume 1: 298–302, New York: Fitzroy Dearborn.

—— (2005) 'Youth Culture, Music and Cell Phone Branding in China', *Global Media and Communication*, 1(2): 185–201.

Warkentin, M., Luo, X. and Templeton, G. (2005) 'A Framework for Spyware Assessment', *Communications of the ACM*, 48(8): 79–84.

Weinberger, D. (2000) 'The Hyperlinked Organization', in R. Levine, C. Locke, C. Searles and D. Weinberger (2000) *The Cluetrain Manifesto. The End of Business as Usual*, Cambridge, MA: Perseus Books.

Wendland, M. (2003) 'The House that Spam Built', *Knowledge, Technology & Policy*, 16(3): 12–15.

Wernick, A. (1991) *Promotional Culture. Advertising, Ideology and Symbolic Expression*, London: Sage.

Winseck, D. (2003) 'Netscapes of Power: Convergence, Network Design, and Other Strategies of Control in the Information Age' in, D. Lyon (ed.) *Surveillance as Social Sorting: Privacy, Risk, and Digital Discrimination*, London: Routledge.

World Bank (2006) 'Overview', in *Information and Communications for Development. Global Trends and Policies*, Washington DC: World Bank. Available at: http://web.worldbank.org/WBSITE/EXTERNAL/TOPICS/EXTINFORMATIONANDCOMMUNICATIONANDTECHNOLOGIES/0,content MDK:20831214~pagePK:210058~piPK:210062~theSitePK:282823,00.html (accessed 22 April 2007).

Yahoo! (1997) *Annual Report*, Financial Section. Available at: http://yhoo.client.shareholder.com/annual.cfm (accessed 6 September 2005).

—— (2000) *Annual Report*, Financial Section F-18. Available at: http://yhoo.client.shareholder.com/annual.cfm (accessed 6 September 2005).

—— (2004) *Annual Report*, Financial Section. Available at: http://yhoo.client.shareholder.com/annual.cfm (accessed 6 September 2005).

Zarsky, T. (2006) 'Online Privacy, Tailoring and Persuasion', in K. Strandburg and D. Raicu (eds) *Privacy and Technologies of Identity. A Cross-Disciplinary Conversation*, New York: Springer.

ZenithOptimedia (2006) 'Online advertising to grow seven times faster than offline advertising in 2007', Press Release, 4 December. Available at: www.zenithoptimedia.com/gff/pdf/Adspend%20forecasts%20December%202006.pdf (accessed 22 March 2007).

Zhang, X. (2005) 'What Do Consumers Really Know about Spyware?', *Communications of the ACM*, 48(8): 44–8.

Zhao, Y. (1998) *Media, Market and Democracy in China. Between the Party Line and the Bottom Line*, Urbana, IL: University of Illinois Press.

Zhou, N. and Belk, R. (2004) 'Chinese Consumer Readings of Global and Local Advertising Appeals', *Journal of Advertising*, Fall: 63–76.

Interviews

Leslie Brydon, Executive Director, Australian Advertising Federation, 24 November 2005, Sydney, Australia.

David Burden, CEO Legion Interactive, 16 August 2004, Sydney, Australia.

Natalie Milnes, Marketing Director, Sensis Interactive, 11 August 2005, Melbourne, Australia (by phone).

Marc Pesce, Lecturer, Interactive Media, Australian Film Television and Radio School, 10 May 2006, Brisbane, Australia.

Jodie Sangster, Legal Director, Australian Direct Marketing Association, 17 June 2005, Sydney, Australia.

Colin Segelov, Executive Director Australian Association of National Advertisers, 23 August 2005, Sydney, Australia.

Duane Varan, Director, Interactive Television Research Institute, Murdoch University, 16 November 2005, Perth, Australia.

Wu Xiaobo, Chariman, PCBP, Interview, 10 September 2004, Beijing, PRC.

Gilbert Yang 2004, Director, Shanghai AdBay, 17 March 2004, Shanghai, PRC.

Index